From the
Candy Store
to the
Galtymore

Stories from Ireland's Showband Era of the 1950s–70s

Dr Joe Kearney — EDITORS — **PJ Cunningham**

Ballpoint Press

To Ricey Scully – for his role in motivating this book – and all his fellow musicians who have lightened Irish lives down the years.

Published in 2017 by Ballpoint Press
4 Wyndham Park, Bray, Co Wicklow, Republic of Ireland.
Telephone: 00353 86 821 7631
Email: ballpointpress1@gmail.com
Web: www.ballpointpress.ie

ISBN 978-0-9954793-5-7

Book design and production by Joe Coyle Media&Design,
joecoyledesign@gmail.com

© Photographs by Michael O'Reilly
and from personal collections

Front Cover: Dancing to Derrick and The Sounds at the Crystal Ballroom,
South Anne Street, Dublin, 12 September, 1968. *Photo by Michael O'Reilly*

Back Cover: Joe Dolan of the Drifters Showband singing to an adoring crowd at the
Television Club, Harcourt Street, Dublin, 20 January, 1969. *Photo by Michael O'Reilly*

Printed and bound by GraphyCems

Contents

	About The Editors	10
	Foreword	11
	Acknowledgements	13
1	The Showband Revolution **Brian D'Arcy**	15
2	A Life-Changing Encounter **Margo O'Donnell**	19
3	The Singing Nun and U2 **Ricey Scully**	25
4	When Horslips Played Through The Night **Pat Belton**	29
5	Sex Outside The Jumper **Billy Keane**	33
6	Paving The Streets Of London **Máire Ní Gioblain**	37
7	Thumbs Up For A Star **John O'Brien**	41
8	'Flower Power' In Callan **Joe Kearney**	43
9	Lucky Escape On Night Of 'Miami Massacre' **Eddie Marmion**	49
10	From The Listening Wall To The Dance Hall **Eileen Casey**	53
11	Minor Miracle In The Early Hours **Ed Cunningham**	57
12	A Royal Dilemma On The Glenshane Pass **Pat Larkin**	61
13	Anthem For An Era... **Kathleen Finan**	65
14	Musical Echoes **James Walsh**	67
15	The Night Bridie Gallagher Played Kilmainham Wood **Pat Cussen**	70
16	Avoiding An Ambush At The GPO **Michael Walsh**	74
17	Sailing For Muff **Brendan Moran**	77
18	The Girl In The Red Coat **Michael Lynch**	80
19	Making An Empty Hall Look Full **Pat Healy**	82
20	Magic Of A First Dance **Pauline Brew**	86
21	Going Back To The Candy Store **Joe King**	89
22	You Can't Trust A Man On A Honda 50 **Gerry Tuohy**	91
23	Playing All Sides With Rebel Kingdom **Michael O'Carroll**	94
24	Blooming At The Rose Of Tralee **Brigid Daly**	95
25	The Hall That Once Was Lives Again **Tom Byrne**	98
26	The Charge Of The Night Brigade **Tom Rowley**	102
27	Running Bear Meets Little White Dove **Collette Bonnar**	106

28   Big In Cadamstown *Brendan Mulhern*   110

29   Scramble In The Ladies Toilet *Seán Halligan*   113

30   Finding Cinderella At The Maple Ballroom *Denis O'Higgins* 116

31   A Window To The Stars *Elaine Bryan*   119

32   A Hair-Raising Tale From 'The Arc' *Rose Hegarty*   121

33   Snowballs And Handbags *Marian Devenish*   124

34   Old Ireland Meets The New In The Bronx *Peter Nolan*   127

35   A Cycle Of Love *Declan P Gowran*   130

36   Bringing The House Down In Manchester *Mildred Beirne*   133

37   Oscar's Last Stand *Mary O'Connor*   136

38   Some Enchanted Evening In Rockcorry *Patricia Cavanagh* 139

39   A 'Welcome Home' From Kelley On My First Date
     Simon Rickard   141

40   A 'Day' That Lasted A Lifetime *Steve Roche*   145

41   Thumbing To Paradise *Maura Flynn*   148

42   Following The Wrong Car Home *Eileen Ludlow*   150

43   Catching The Wave *David Fegan*   153

44   Marching To The Same Beat *Cathal Gunning*   156

45   Ballroom Of Romance How Are Ya! *Maeve Edwards*   160

46   Jack The Lad *Tom Aherne*   163

47   The Buckled Wheel *Tony McCormack*   165

48   Thumbing When The Chips Were Down
     Rosemary McDermott   168

49   Butch Moore's Green Field Shock *Fred Molloy*   171

50   Little Arrows *Bayveen O'Connell*   174

51   Looking For The Shift *Maurice Crowley*   176

52   A Hunger For Love – And Food *Monica Fitzell*   179

53   The Ghost Of Dickie Rock *Ron Woods*   181

54   The Magic Of The Banba *Catherine Murphy*   186

55   Future Taoiseach Comes To Our Rescue *Neil Owens*   189

56   The Art Of Free Admission To Dances *Peter Gordon*   191

57   Crash, Bang, Wallop At 'The Arc' *Bunty Flynn*   194

58   Stiletto Heels And The Melody Aces *Betty Devenney*   197

59   Some Dance To Remember, I Danced To Forget *Joan Griffin*   200

60 A Diabolical Intervention Or Divine Inspiration? *Joe Keane* 203

61 Dedicated Follower (Of The Wrong) Fashion
Lorna Sixsmith 206

62 The Fight For A Fair Lady *Mark McGaugh* 210

63 Bright Lights That Failed To Shine *Paul Holland* 213

64 Hanging Out With The Rockers *Anne Lacey* 215

65 From Céilí To Carnival Girl *Frances Browner* 218

66 Back To Front For Luck! *Monica Weir* 222

67 Falling Into The Wrong Hands *Seán Burns* 225

68 Tunnels, Skeletons And Wellington Boots
Victor Sandilands 228

69 Something In The Air *PJ Cunningham* 230

70 Friday Night At The Fiesta *Moira Gallagher* 235

71 The Lovely Grá Mo Chroí *Joe McShane/Margo O'Donnell* 237

Also by Ballpoint Press 239

About The Editors

PJ Cunningham

PJ is an editor, publisher and journalist who is also the author of the trilogy, *The Lie of the Land*, *A Fly Never Lit* and *The Long Acre*, which was shortlisted for Irish Book Of The Year in 2014.

He also wrote *A.N. Other* in 2001 and has written and edited *Around The Farm Gate* and co-edited *Then There Was Light*.

A native of Clara, Co Offaly, PJ now lives in Bray, Co Wicklow with his wife Rosemary and family of five.

Dr Joe Kearney

Joe is a writer, broadcaster and multi-award-winning documentary maker. His short fiction has been published in many anthologies and one of his stories was a finalist in the Francis MacManus awards.

He holds a PhD in creative writing from UCD and is a native of Callan, Co Kilkenny but now lives in Enniskerry, Co Wicklow with his wife Anne.

He is an inveterate storyteller, with a keen ear for the off-beat and the curious.

He co-edited *Then There Was Light* in 2016.

Foreword

THE nineteen fifties to the seventies was a seminal time in Ireland's social development as showbands brought a cultural revolution to every corner of the country.

As De Valera's comely maidens exited the village greens, a new, brash and more vibrant culture came along with a wider universal influence.

Bill Haley, Elvis and later The Beatles and Rolling Stones replaced the more staid set-dance and céilí environment that had prevailed for generations.

The emergence of a host of celebrity showbands saw a massive increase in the number of dancehalls springing up to cater for the huge numbers that religiously followed these new bands.

Dickie Rock, Brendan Bowyer, Butch Moore, Joe Dolan, Big Tom, Larry Cunningham, Margo, Eileen Reid, Kelley and Philomena Begley – to name but a few – didn't just provide entertainment for the star-struck young dancers; they gave them a place and a reason to meet and oftentimes find a lifelong partner.

And not just in Ireland. The showbands became an integral part of the lives of Irish people domiciled in communities in Britain due to economic necessity. These exiles formed a bond with the Irish bands who brought a little bit of Irish living to venues all over Britain.

As one person aptly put it: "I stepped out of the door of the Mayfair Ballroom in Kilkenny and walked seamlessly through the front doors of the Galtymore." The dancehall sustained that generation and satisfied the need for "home" that is in every Irish person forced to leave these shores.

This book has been a real joy for us to work on because it allowed us a unique opportunity to write down the compelling stories from so many diverse social perspectives.

Dr Joe Kearney and PJ Cunningham
September 2017

Acknowledgements

W E would like to sincerely thank the hundreds of people who got in touch with us to tell us their stories or simply wish us luck with our undertaking.

There has been a huge groundswell of support for this book on both sides of the Irish Sea and it is our hope that the following pages will act as a lens for future generations to see how the Irish people of the showband era lived and loved.

The contemporary music industry owes a huge debt of gratitude to those pioneering bands who criss-crossed the country to bring dancing joy to hundreds of thousands of young Irish people.

The contribution of those bands to Irish life was both groundbreaking and pivotal in the shaping of a more contemporary nation. Those stars became musical royalty and still hold a special place of fondness in our hearts decades down the line from those halcyon days and nights.

We received contact and in some cases submissions from many more people than one volume of work could cater for. We would like to sincerely acknowledge all those who we were unable to include on this occasion.

Lastly, a sincere word of thanks to both our families for the help and encouragement they gave us during the compiling, writing, editing and production of *From The Candy Store To The Galtymore*.

They agreed to organise a competition in the hall that night to find a name for the band, with the winner getting half a crown. Various people wrote suggestions on the back of cigarette packets. One of them was: 'The Sweet Afton Band – because there's not a player among you.'

The Showband
Revolution

Brian D'Arcy

I'M often asked to tell the story of the Showband era in Ireland. It's funny when what was once central to my life, is now a history lesson, little more than a memory.

What I'm writing here isn't a complete history of a hugely exciting era, but a selection of random anecdotes in an attempt to share a flavour of what was an exciting, almost revolutionary, period.

The Clipper Carlton was the first showband ever. And it came about, as most good things do, by accident. They were from Strabane in County Tyrone. There was a man called Hughie Toorish who had a band in that area. They were a typical band in those days. They dressed in dickey-bows, black suits and white shirts and they sat behind music stands playing everything in strict tempo. Toorish was the leader of the band and the piano player. In an interview, he described them well: "We were like undertakers arriving for a dance."

They were not a showband yet. They went one night to Fintona in County Tyrone, in the early '50s. The local priest, Fr Carty, who was raising money for the parish, said: "Why don't you get a proper name? Call yourselves something else." They agreed to organise a competition in the hall that night to find a name for the band with the winner getting half a crown. Various people wrote suggestions on the back of cigarette packets. One of them was: "The Sweet Afton Band-because there's not a player among you."

Another suggestion was "The Clipper Carlton Band." Clipper was the name given to American planes during the Second World War, which landed on Lough Erne. They created this image of flying across the Atlantic, it was daring, different and glamorous. They won the half a crown.

They began including a variety interval in their dance music. On an occasion when they were booked to perform in Dundalk, an enterprising proprietor saw an opening for something new. He advertised them on a wall 'Playing tonight: The Clipper Carlton Showband.' The name stuck with them. That's how an industry began.

The Clipper Carlton were out on their own. They had their instruments highly polished and well presented. They worked out a show which entertained people even when they weren't dancing. They were the first to throw away music stands and to stand up for the entire night. They brought excitement and a whole new world to the people of Ireland. Others followed and surpassed them but they were the pioneers.

Elvis was the up and coming star at the time, music changed and they were like travelling juke boxes, introducing pop stars of the world to the most rural parts of Ireland. The clergy were slow to change. The Clippers told me they travelled from Strabane to Kerry for a dance. Of course, people hadn't got used to that sort of a band in the different regions of the country.

In Kerry, Mickey O'Hanlon was drumming. All he could see from his position on stage were bicycles going by him. He couldn't figure it out. There was a room at the back of the stage where the people could park their bicycles for safety. They came into the hall, paid their money, rode their bikes up the hall and parked them at the back.

There was a priest in the area who had this idea that music raised the passions too easily at dances. He instructed them that, after every three songs they were to stop for precisely two minutes. He stood at the edge of the stage all night with his stop watch in hand. At the end of the set, he'd say: "Wait for two minutes," and at the end of the two minutes he'd shout: "go now." That was his way of keeping his parishioners' passions under control.

There was a time when the transition from local bands in local halls to showbands who travelled the length and breadth of the country overlapped. Members of the Mighty Avons Showband remember country halls where people threw paraffin oil on the floor to make it slippy. Can you imagine what a fire hazard that was? In those days people smoked non-stop in the dance halls. You could see a blue haze of smoke rising from the hall as the nights went on.

The Royal Showband were another band who pioneered new markets. Making records was one of them. The first showband record was released

54 years ago this year, in 1963. Since there were no studios here, the Royal Showband had to go to England and record in the Abbey Road studios, the same place that the Beatles recorded some of their greatest songs.

Mentioning the Beatles and showbands reminds me of a story which Brendan Bowyer recalled clearly. The Royal had just won the Carl Allen Award for being the best band in Britain and Ireland. As a result, they were touring England. When they came to play in Liverpool there was a young band keeping the audience entertained until they came on stage. The young band was the early Beatles. Brendan remembered how Lennon and McCartney came to look at their luxury wagon. They wondered aloud if they'd ever make enough money to buy a bus like that. Brendan advised them to keep writing their own songs and they might.

Elvis Presley admired the talents of the Royal Showband. Late at night he often went to see them perform after his own show. One of the highlights of the show was Brendan Bowyer doing an imitation of Elvis Presley. Elvis loved that part of the show.

The Mighty Avons were the first showband to have a record in the top 10 in the British charts. Jim Reeves was a famous country singer who was adored in Ireland. When he died in a plane crash in 1964, the late Eddie Masterson had a song written within five minutes on the inside of a Sweet Afton packet. He convinced the Avons to record it and they eventually did. It went into the Top 10 in the British pop charts.

I don't know when it was that I realised how important showbands were to the people of Ireland. Like most things in life I didn't appreciate them when they were in their heyday. At least I didn't appreciate the contribution they made to modernising Ireland.

If I were asked to say when the "Golden Age" declined, I would have to say it was when the Miami Showband were murdered. That's when the fun ended. The Miami massacre was tragic for a number of reasons, the main one being the death of three lovely, talented musicians.

The Miami Showband was truly a mixed band. There were Catholics and Protestants in the band. There were northerners and southerners in the band. There was one from Cork and one from Ballymena. It was just about the most perfect mix you could get in a band. If you were going to attack a band for sectarian reasons, the Miami was the worst choice you could make.

For me, the Miami massacre was the day the music died. It was the day innocence died. The showband scene never recovered from it. Many of the big bands stopped going north. The entertainment scene changed completely. The innocence of the whole showband era which had been thriving since 1955. It was a sad time but like life, everything changed and moved on.

Brian D'Arcy is one of Ireland's best-known and best-loved priests. A native of Bellanaleck, Co Fermanagh, he has been the unofficial chaplain to the showbusiness community for over 40 years. He is the author of several books as well as being a columnist for the 'Sunday World' and broadcaster on BBC.

A Life-changing Encounter

Margo O'Donnell

I'VE seen every side of the showband scene in my time and I'm happy to have lived to tell the tale.

It was a great and exciting time to be part of, but with the laughter there were tears along the way. Not just for me but for many people in it.

Of course there was a lot of fun too. It was a new time in Ireland's social and cultural lifetime and we were at the heart of it.

And it wasn't just in this country; the Irish in Britain were as much part of that social revolution as those who stayed at home.

I was lucky to get to see so much of that first hand when the band would go on tours to England or Scotland. That happened mostly around Lent when the parish priests in Ireland would earmark that time for prayer and reflection rather than singing and dancing.

I started out on that trek initially in 1964, though it was 1967 before I got to sing in the Galtymore and the Gresham ballrooms for the first time. That's a full 50 years ago and I still have fantastic memories of playing all those UK venues.

There were Irish dancehalls all over London...The Forum in Kentish Town, the 32 Club in Harlesden, the Harp in New Cross. And then there was a lot of smaller halls as well and the Catholic clubs were venues which we would play in off-nights away from the big dances on Saturday and, believe it or not, Monday nights. You could be booked to play for a whole week in the London area during Lent.

I suppose the 'Galty' is the one place that sticks out mostly because it was more than a ballroom to the Irish in London. It was a meeting place and an institution for the exiled youth and has rightly become part of our folklore.

As well as singing there countless times, I think I also attended four or five wedding receptions in the place. It was usually a case that the bride and groom met there at a dance, then got married and held their reception and later had their children's christening there as well.

The Galtymore has so much of a story to tell us about Irish culture and history of that era in particular and here are a few different tales of mine.

I remember one night I was singing in the old hall and these two fellas down to my left started beating the lard out of each other. Some sort of scuffle was part of the culture of those dancing nights. As they'd say a little tongue in cheek at home – "a night out was no good without a fight."

I have other vivid memories too. I remember going over in the late sixties and early seventies and bringing clothes for people from around home. I also brought over homemade brown bread from a neighbour who called up with the freshly baked cakes and told me she had told her son he could collect them at the bandstand.

Probably the biggest laugh I got was one night in the Gresham, when one of the bouncers said there was a fella outside with a big box. They wouldn't let him in but he insisted that he had to talk to me.

I went down because I knew him. Sure enough, there he was with a huge package in front of him. I said to him: "What have you there?" He said he wanted his mother to have the first microwave oven in Donegal and would I bring it home to her?

I was Ireland's answer to Fed Ex but was happy to oblige anyone when they asked me. I brought money home that young people gave me to give to their families. There were times when it worked the other way as well. A fella from my home got sick and I took money over from his parents. This was part of life.

The most abiding memory I have though is a story that is quite different to any of the others – it is one of triumph over tragedy, one where someone who had fallen on hard times recovered to discover his dignity before dying.

I was heading down to sing in one of those in-between nights at a little Catholic club located somewhere between Hammersmith and Fulham.

I heard a voice call out my name in what I could best describe as a loud whisper from the alleyway beside the hall. For a second I thought I was imagining it but then I heard the voice say 'Margo' again.

In the darkness I made out the form of a homeless man sitting on the pavement. I had seen several Irish lads like him who had fallen on hard times. You'd come across lots of them from the same backgrounds as ourselves in that part of Cricklewood High Road. He told me he'd been trying to get in to the dance but the caretaker refused him admission.

"I've no money," he explained, "but I just wanted to go in to hear you sing 'A Gra mo Chroi' and 'At the Close of an Irish Day.'" That song was very popular at the time for Bridie Gallagher. I assured him that I'd work something out and went in to talk to the caretaker. I told him I'd vouch for the man – who was originally from the west of Ireland. I explained that he wouldn't cause any trouble and suggested that he could be accommodated up on a little balcony at the end of the hall.

The caretaker relented and the man, whose names was James, came in. I bought him a glass of Guinness and left it up there with him while I did the show. After the dance I went across the road to a chipper and got him sausages and chips and brought them back to him.

When I asked him where he was staying for the night, he told me he was bedding down in the alley where I'd found him earlier.

I was due to go home the next day but decided against it. Instead, I contacted the Irish Centre in Camden town and got him in to one of their places. I also got the opportunity to talk further to James who told me his story about taking to the drink and being unable to give it up.

"But I want to give it up, Margo," he said with a steely determination. I resolved to do my best to help him get back to Ireland. Fortunately I managed to find accommodation for him in a therapeutic place. I then returned to England so we could both travel back together. When he went inside this place they undertook a thorough medical on him and unfortunately discovered that he had cancer. He was given six months to live.

His own overriding wish was to stop drinking so that he could die sober. It was great credit to him, God rest his soul, that he did stop and was sober for the last three months of his life.

It meant something to him that he was able to die in that manner.

I can tell you that James was indeed proud and upright and a good man again in his own eyes, and I felt privileged to be there with him when he died.

Of course, it was sad seeing him go but there was also something uplifting about the victory he experienced by raising himself out of the gutter to stand tall again before he passed away.

I feel incredibly lucky to have met that man. I only knew him really for a few months but the impact of meeting him and getting to know him and his story has empowered me for the rest of my own life. You could say it had a very profound effect on me.

It was a personal thing and I didn't talk about it to anybody for years. It was something between himself and myself and besides he didn't want anyone to know about his situation. I was happy to keep it that way. He was a human being, somebody's son, somebody's brother and as I said, he was a very proud person.

The encounter with James meant a lot more to me because of my own drink problem. I suppose I approached his case with a lot more understanding of where he was and what he was thinking because I had once been there myself.

And I knew that when he was at the stage of reaching out to somebody – me – looking for help, he was ripe to receive it. I was able to assist him because I had been helped myself.

We talked about many things during the months before he passed away. One of the funniest chats we had was when we discussed how much alcohol each of us would consume in a session. When I told him my intake, he scoffed: "Sure you weren't a proper drinker at all. I spilt more than you were able to drink."

Of course, it's not the amount you drink that's the problem, it's what it does to you. How it changes you, your personality and your relationships with others.

I know how lucky I was to get help and standing there outside the hall in the alleyway that night, I thought to myself when I looked at him... "there but for the grace of God." I was very honoured James allowed me to be his friend. Since then, it has kept me grounded. It's now a long, long time since I took a drink and I'm happy to say that it doesn't bother me any longer.

However I know I wasn't typical. I've never admitted this publicly before but the reason I drank was because I was afraid of the stage. The terror stemmed from the fact that I was a very young girl when I started out singing and had many, many bad experiences in the music business.

I felt I had no choice but to work to help my mother raise the family. She needed me and I almost killed myself in the process.

My father had just died and I was a young one who trusted everybody. I had a terrible time in the business with people taking advantage of my situation.

I could see that I was being sold short and to cover up my fears and unhappiness, I turned to drink. I found when I took refuge there it shielded me from my thoughts. It anaesthetised me from the world and it allowed me to go on and perform because I wouldn't think about what was happening and consequently didn't feel as afraid. I'm glad to say I'm no longer afraid of the stage. But back then, that's what it did to me.

I decided to tell James story not for anyone to say 'Good on ya, Margo.' I wanted to celebrate how this down-at-heel human being got up off his knees and walked tall again.

It took me years before I decided I should share it. I arrived at that conclusion because it struck me that some other people in similar predicaments might hear James' story and maybe it would give them the encouragement they were looking for to confront their problem? Eventually I spoke to my mother about it and she said to tell it. In fact she believed that I should have told it years before.

The morning we buried James, there was no on there but myself, the undertaker and one or two from the centre. That scene of a few people huddled together at the grave will live with me forever. And I know if I never do anything in my life, at least I will have been witness to seeing a good end for a proud man who took himself off to London to make something of himself – but it didn't work out.

He was one of the thousands who left our shores with hope in their hearts and happened to suffer along the way. We reflected those emotions in the words of songs we sang at that time – tales of hardship and heartache, loneliness and loss, of demons and drink, of life and death.

They were the songs we sang back then and they're the songs we're still singing today. They were once the young people who walked the roads to come to hear Big Tom, Philomena Begley, Brian Coll, myself and dozens of other bands who were a link between them and home.

And their children are still listening to them today.

Margo O'Donnell has been the recognised Queen of Country & Irish for a generation of Irish music and dance lovers on both sides of the Irish Sea, as well as Australia and America. A native of Co Donegal, she now lives in Co Monaghan. She co-wrote the lyrics of 'The Lovely Grá Mo Chroí' with Joe McShane to recall her meeting with 'James' in the above story. (See lyrics on Page 237)

*We had one big challenge –
how to get our hands on a
pair of nuns' habits. That
week we were due to play in
The Dell in Athlone and we
wanted to have this novelty
act ready for the big occasion*

3

The Singing Nun and U2

Ricey Scully

THE music industry has many faces and I washed most of them during my half century either performing or organising bands for the stage.

When I was growing up in Clara, Co Offaly, it seemed that every second household in the little town had someone in a band. There was the legendary Jimmy Rabbitte and his band and later the Countrymen and The Crackaways who appeared on an RTÉ television show in the mid-sixties. No one talked about anything else for weeks afterwards.

As the years went by I was involved with various groups, usually driving them in Jackie Rabbitte's minibus to the gig, then playing tin whistle, saxophone and singing before packing up the gear and heading home after the ball was over.

No gimmick was off limits. When the 'Singing Nun' came along with 'Dominique' in the sixties, myself and my fellow band member Mickey Kenny, who unfortunately passed away earlier this year, decided to make it an attraction in our show.

Everyone was singing the song back then – it was a hit in the charts in the US, UK and in Ireland.

We had one big challenge – how to get our hands on a pair of nuns' habits. That week we were due to play in The Dell in Athlone and we wanted to have this novelty act ready for the big occasion.

We decided that we couldn't afford to get them made in a tailor's shop so we approached the local convent with more than a little trepidation to ask the nuns if they had any spare habits.

The impression of nuns at that time was that they were holy people who wouldn't play ball with this sort of secular activity.

In reality, the opposite was the case. Not only did they help to dress us up, they even put make-up on us wherever they found it.

When we were ready to leave the convent, all the nuns applauded us as we made our way out to the minibus. We had hardly driven a hundred yards out the gate when we met the parish priest on the road as he was indicating to turn into the Parochial House. He nearly crashed the car when he saw 'two nuns' waving at him as they drove past him.

We had earlier arranged with the rest of the band that we would make a 'grand entrance' to the venue when we got to Athlone. Mickey was to take to the stage in his recently acquired nun's habit and sing "Dominique." Then, when the song was over I would make my entrance shouting: 'I'm the reverend mother, has anyone seen a singing nun?"

Unfortunately, while I sat out in the van, I didn't realise that there was a bit of a delay. Waiting inside, Mickey reckoned he had time to nip to the loo before the performance. However he forgot that he had changed sex and burst into the 'Gents' to spend a penny.

The three punters who were inside the toilet nearly had a heart attack when they turned around to see the vision of a nun behind them lifting her habit.

It was exactly at that time that I entered to see what was going on. On entry, I asked the two lads as they came rushing out: "Did you see a singing Nun anywhere?"

"Yes, but right now she's a pee-ing nun," one of them replied. "And she's still in the Gents if you don't believe me," he added.

* * *

When it came to music I was prepared to turn my hand to nearly anything so when the opportunity arose many years later for me to run a venue, I took it. It had recently been rechristened 'The Garden of Eden' (it was formerly the Central Ballroom in Tullamore).

At that time – the late seventies – the golden days of ballrooms were slipping away but there was still a business there. Changing the name of the venue was part of that changing scene. Obviously you paid the big names big bucks but for the lesser groups, I usually paid bands £500-£600 per gig. I became astute at knowing which bands would make a profit for all concerned and which ones might be borderline cases or worse still, loss-makers.

And I worked off good advice such as that given to me by the legendary TJ Byrne, the manager of the Royal Showband. He told me to make sure

I did my sums in advance and particularly if there was a cleric involved. He recalled the time a very charming Parish Priest had inveigled him to bring the Royal down to a place on the west coast with the promise that "they would be well looked after."

As they travelled down, TJ admitted to the lads in the band that he didn't know how much they would be getting that night. He went on: "I won't tell you the place but I knew shortly after we arrived that I had made a big mistake. The PP went up onto the stage to thank me and the lads for what we were doing for his parish. He then explained that as a mark of appreciation, seven women in the parish had knitted aran sweaters for each member of the band and his own housekeeper had knitted one for me. They were hanging out of the rafters that night and a lot of money had been handed over at the admission booth but we didn't see a penny for our troubles," he explained.

Thereafter TJ championed that the day you did the booking was the day you tied down all the loose ends. It was a lesson that I never forgot.

So when I was approached to see if I would book a group called U2, I felt I would be taking a chance as they weren't that big a draw. In fact no one down our way had heard of them. My friend in the business from Dublin, Noel Carty, said I'd be alright as the usual crowd would turn up on a Sunday night anyway. It was with a little reluctance that finally I agreed but instead of giving them the normal fee, I said I would pay them £100 less. That way I was making it easier for the finances to work out.

Unfortunately my hunch was correct. On the night U2 attracted only a fair to middling size crowd into the hall despite the decision to reduce the admission price by half. My over-riding memory of the performance of Bono and the boys was the bouncers approaching me half way through the night complaining that the band was so loud they were going out for a while to give their ears a rest.

The man who became a legend in the business, Paul McGuinness, was there that night as U2's fledgling manager. Paul obviously had a prescience that was way above my head. As I handed over the money at the end of the night, we struck up the usual small talk around the world of music.

I admired the total optimism he had about the band. We looked out at them as they performed their last number. He saw stardom ahead, I saw a small knot of people looking up from the dance floor.

"These guys are destined for the very top," he assured me enthusiastically. "We have the financial backing and they'll soon be playing the big venues of the world."

I couldn't contain myself. "Yea, that might very well be the case, but I can guarantee you one thing, they won't be playing the Garden of Eden again."

I get it hard to tell this story without laughing now. And there was even a funny postscript to the above encounter.

Many, many years later – and by the way I became a big U2 fan both for their music and how they have represented Ireland – I was listening to an interview Bono was giving to some American TV station.

The interviewer talked about the various albums and the tours and the fans and ended his programme with this question: "Tell me, Bono, where would you be today if U2 hadn't become the global brand you now are."

Bono was silent for a second and then answered: "Well, if we hadn't made it the way we did, I think we'd still be in the Garden of Eden."

Ricey Scully is a well-known music figure in the midlands. He is married with four grown-up children. A former Offaly footballer and hurler from the 1960s, he still loves listening to music and performs occasionally.

4

When Horslips Played Through The Night

Pat Belton

HORSLIPS weren't just another band of the 1970s – they represented a new music movement for a generation of Celtic rock fans.

Young people of that time followed them the length and breadth of the country – sometimes camping out to ensure that they got to see the group without having to pay the earth in accommodation.

Back then, I was involved in the music industry, I had my own disco show where I played relief to big acts around the country but more particularly in the Longford and Midlands area.

I also began to do some promotional work – now I was no Jim Aiken but I knew how to promote a concert. And I certainly did that when I managed to book Horslips to play in Ardagh Community Hall one weekend in the mid 1970s.

These new premises had just been built by the Local Development Committee and financed largely from running the very successful Ardagh Carnival over many years. It opened on Easter Sunday night each year, usually with Tommy & Jimmy Swarbrigg and The Times playing to crowds in excess of 1,500 in a five-pole marquee.

Now news that Horslips were coming to our area created even greater excitement in the whole of the midlands; we knew we had another sellout on our hands. On the night, I was in the perfect position to oversee everything as I was the DJ and disco until the group came on stage. My then girlfriend Valerie (now my wife) was in charge of the Box Office and we weren't at all surprised that the new hall was packed from very early on. A huge number of Horslips devotees had camped in the village on the previous night and helped to create an electric buzz around the place which continued through the Saturday and into the evening time.

A great crowd. A great band. A great atmosphere. What could possibly go wrong?

The alarm bells began ringing in my ears when I hadn't seen the usual signs of a group arriving – a lorry with roadies and the band's equipment. I was also at a loss that the great Horslips manager, Michael Deeney, hadn't shown up.

Obviously I was working on stage and got it hard to convey my mounting concern. All I could do was work on the presumption that they would turn up. Between records I kept assuring the fans that it wouldn't be long now until their heroes arrived to play for them.

What happened in the following eight hours or so was both the most frightening and exhilarating period of my life. As the clock ticked on past half 10 to 11 o'clock, I knew something was definitely wrong. I alerted Valerie and the staff that we should start phoning to see if we could find out where they were.

Now the seventies was a time when there were no mobiles/social media so communication was not like it is today, but fortunately I was able to contact a friend of Michael Deeney's ...and then discovered everything.

There was a simple explanation for Horslips 'no show' in our village that night. When the booking was made, Michael was under the impression that the band would be playing in Arva – not Ardagh, and their equipment wagon and roadies and, of course, the band arrived in the Co Cavan town in plenty of time.

There the locals told them that there was no one due to play in the Arva Hall that night. Believing that they had a phantom booking on their hands, the entire entourage adjourned to a local pub with a view to relaxing now that work was off the menu.

The following few hours became for me the miracle of Ardagh. It was approaching midnight when Michael arrived in his Range Rover, wearing a three-quarter-length coat which all hardened rockers wore at that time.

Michael was very professional and said they would honour the contract to play. I told the fans about the mix-up and they were over the moon when I explained that true to form, Horslips wouldn't let them down. However I warned that it would still take some time before they could get on stage.

It was about 25 miles between the two similar sounding places – Arva to Ardagh – and the equipment had to be transported and then put up on the stage before the usual checking for sound and feedback could be done.

In the heel of the hunt, we finally got Horslips playing in Ardagh at 2am – the time when normally they would finish.

I don't suppose they ever got a better reception than when they hit the stage in Ardagh that night or more accurately in the early hours of the following morning.

The fans went wild and somehow a bond was created between both sides. So much so that it was six o'clock in the morning when Amhrán na Bhfhiann rang out and much later when people dispersed.

Michael had long gone and I could get no one in the band who would accept payment. That's the sort of lads they were – they loved the music and playing and money was only secondary. It meant I had to meet Michael in Dublin later the following week to pay him.

Back in Ardagh, Horslips were on everyone's lips. Even after they finished playing, the musicians stayed around talking to the fans and this was noted by the early risers making their way to first mass on the Sunday morning.

It emerged very quickly that not everyone was enamoured with the sound of Dearg Doom, Charolais and Flower Among Them All being belted out as people were home in their beds trying to sleep.

The Parish Priest at Sunday morning mass denounced the all-night "racket from the Horsey band" and social media or no social media, his comments made it to the front page of the Longford Leader's next edition and to the following week's Sunday Independent where it was displayed under the slightly racier headline – 'PP slates the Horsey band'.

And of course there was irony in the mix too. One woman was irate at the all-night carry on, and loudly complained – "What's become of the youth today?"

Fortunately, she never recognised that the young man in the Leader photograph who was snapped naked to the waist – but had his hands up hiding his face while playing his 'air guitar' – was none other than her son who, as it turned out, would go on to become a leading figure in society.

Pat Belton is a native of Ardagh, Co Longford and has worked in the music business in the 70s and early 80s.

The girls of our age didn't wear high heels. It was the men who were falling down steps and saying stuff like "my feet are killing me" or "I can't wait to get home and take these off."

5

Sex Outside The Jumper

Billy Keane

OLD men sucked smoke from pipes the length of glockenspiels and solemnly declared the wearing of the long hair was the advent of the end of the ancient civilization of the Gael.

We grew the hair down to our shoulders, or in my case there was a beehive hut constructed on top of my head. Think Phil Lynott and that was me back then. Thin Lizzie was the sound in our ballroom of romance. The solid men who went to the regular dances had their hair sheared tighter than a hedgehog heading for a job interview. These men arrived to the dance dressed up in their good suits, with white shirts and knots in their ties as big as mangles. And they too were being interviewed ... by the girls.

We were the late arrivals and in the mid-seventies our football team led the way. Every one of the mighty Kerry team of the seventies and eighties sported long locks.

At the beginning there was consternation from the men who ate bacon and cabbage 363 days a year. There was turkey on Christmas Day and St Stephen's Day back when the bird, as it was known, was larger than a pterodactyl.

The solid men were set in their ways and when young lads togged out for the local football team with hair longer than their sisters and mothers, there was terrible criticism if you kicked a wide.

When the Kerry team started winning All Irelands the hair length was of no consequence and us young lads were alright then. All was forgiven and we got in under the county team amnesty.

I remember so well hitching off to Ballybunion with the lads. I was a big man back in the seventies. The beehive hut put a few inches on to me and the platform shoes were scaffolding. The girls of our age didn't wear high heels. It was the men who were falling down steps and saying stuff like "my feet are killing me" or "I can't wait to get home and take these off."

There wasn't much sex though in the country places. It was a big thrill to get what was known as a bit of "outside the jumper". There were many who were sure men and women had the same reproductive organs as the rabbit. The biology teacher used this diagram of the rabbit to explain the facts of life.

A survivor explained it all. "If you asked your father about sex education, he'd say: "Ask your mother." And she'd say: "Didn't they teach ye that at school?" And then your father would come back to you and say: "Don't be upsetting your mother" when you asked her about how's your father."

People learned on the job, so to speak, and Playboy was smuggled in from England by lads who stuck the magazine under their jumpers coming through customs for fear of confiscation.

An old doctor told me he had a patient who couldn't figure out how it was she was pregnant for the sixth time. The doctor said the only form of contraception was "to keep your two legs in the one stocking."

And we had fierce hard luck. For some unaccountable reason the mini-skirt went out of fashion and women wore maxis down past the knees on more formal occasions. For the dances everyone wore blue jeans. And if you were to look at someone from behind there was no great difference other than the women had nicer bottoms.

I'm not quite sure whether or not a marquee could be classified as a ballroom but I do recall a night at Finuge when the ladies toilets collapsed during a particularly lively version of Margo's 'Blanket on the Ground'.

The toilets were a sheet of suspended tarpaulin and 3,000 people jumping up and down at the same time had the very same effect as a quake on the San Andreas fault.

The urgent rearrangement of undergarments was like when the husband walks in on his wife and the postman.

There was lots of what was called shifting. Men always made the first move. It was considered un-ladylike for a woman to initiate the shifting.

The shifting was hit badly when The Pope came to Ireland in 1978. There was an outbreak of religious fervour which led to a rise in chastity and modesty.

But sometimes nature took its course and most of the young girls had to put their babies up for adoption in times when society was very hard on women who got pregnant outside marriage.

My favourite band was Horslips and they played Celtic rock. We loved the Celtic Rock. I had to miss a Horslips gig in Ballybunion because I had to work in our pub. It broke my heart.

I asked my friend Donncha if it was a good night. He was a bit put out because I was his wing man and he had to look after two girls on his own.

"Were Horslips only brilliant?" I asked.

"They were that good," replied Donncha, "that there was this lad from Moyvane who got so excited, he got an electric shock from his air guitar."

The Moyvane boys, the Brosna gang and the Koncknagoshel lads too, were all going around calling each other "man." Some of the boys even called the women "man." There were many girls who didn't like all the noise but these were mostly ones with buttons missing in their cardigans. And the chat up line of "what kind of music do you like was answered by "I do melt when I hear Larry Gogan on the radio." DJ Larry always kept up with the times.

Then one Sunday night the older lads on our football team persuaded us to go to Maurice Mulcahy and his Orchestra in the Central Ballroom.

We stood out in our jackets, jeans and platforms. One lad came up to me after staring for a good 10 minutes and asked if I was a hippy. "No" I replied, "I'm a Keane."

So us young lads stayed up on the balcony jeering at the straight-laced, some of whom danced with our mothers and even our grandmothers.

This oul' lad who was old enough to have fought in the GPO came over to me with a gleam in his eye. He was wearing a parcel from America purple suit hemming in a Cinzano Bianco red and yellow Manhattan cabaret shirt. He asked if I was "young Keane".

"I was the last time I checked my birth cert."

Us townies were full of smart answers. The old boy ignored me. He was on a mission. "Is your grandmother going with anyone? Tell her I'm interested."

But then the music won us over. There was a brass section and trumpets. Glenn Miller's Little Brown Jug shut us up. The sound was universal and we were entranced almost surreptitiously by the majesty of the playing.

Years later, in a pub in Clonmel, I told Maurice Mulcahy of the night he converted the North Kerry School of Rock to the big band sound. He smiled, gave me one of his tapes and I still have it.

But a few days later the boys were back in town. Thin Lizzie brought out 'Whiskey in the Jar' and 3,000 of us were playing air guitar on our knees with mad shaking of our heads like the young one the devil got at in The Exorcist.

I spotted a beautiful young girl and I said to the lads "some day that girl over there will be my wife." But it was not to be. I was refused the dance with a shake of the head. There wasn't even a "no thanks" or an "ask my sister, I'm sweatin'."

She went off with a big farmer's son from the lush pasture lands of the Golden Vale. I didn't even get to talk to her.

However five minutes later I was in love with someone else and five minutes after that someone else again. The music was different, the clothes and the hair too, but we were still dancing in the Ballroom of Romance.

Billy Keane is a well-known Listowel publican who is also a top columnist with the 'Irish Independent'. Married with four children, he is the author of a number of best-selling books, including his novel, 'The Last Of The Heroes' and a collection of his newspapers writings entitled, 'The Best of Billy Keane'.

6

Paving The
Streets Of London

Máire Ní Gioblain

THEY say you can always spot a tourist in large cities; they are the ones who constantly look up, who seldom look straight ahead and who rarely look at the pavement.

Not me though – I'm one of those who always look down at where I am stepping. You see when I walk the streets of London there is a chance that I am placing my feet on part of my late husband's legacy. Tim was a master paver at the very highest end of his craft. When he died they said that if he was not the best in Britain then definitely he was the best in London.

If the Irish built Britain after WW2, then Tim paved its walkways, streets and paths. He was proud of what he did. In Hollywood, the famous get to have their name and a star inscribed onto the pavement. You won't find my husband's name inscribed on anything other than his tombstone, which is why I always look down when I walk in the city because I know I am stepping on his work.

In some ways it seems ironic that I am stepping upon him, as the first time we met and danced together in the Galtymore in Cricklewood, it was he who stepped on me. Most of the Irish lads who danced there worked hard and enjoyed a drink. Tim was one of those and maybe that accounted for his faulty choreography the night we danced together in the céilí section of the dancehall.

My sister Nora and I had been attending the weekend dances there from the time we arrived in London. We were there in the early 60s when no alcohol was sold in the Galtymore. They didn't get a licence until years later. In those early days we moved between the Céilí and the Showband sections depending on whatever humour was upon us. We similarly moved between rented rooms around Neasden, Queens Park, Kilburn and, of course, Cricklewood. Like many other Irish women. I worked in hospitals, stores and factories. There was never a shortage of employment and we were young and Nora and I looked out for each other. At the dances when no one asked us up we'd dance with each other and when no one asked to accompany us home we went home with each other.

I recall one night when I had met a lad who wanted to see me home. I explained I was there with my sister but he declared that this was no problem as he could arrange transport. He left us standing outside the 'Galty' and disappeared along Cricklewood Broadway. We watched him go through the junction and the traffic lights and then disappear into the Crown car park. The sister nudged me and winked: "He has a car."

Moments later we saw him appear wheeling a pushbike. He graciously proffered it to my sister and suggested that she cycle back to the bedsit in Kilburn and that he would walk me home himself. He offered to lower the saddle for her.

Needless to say we thanked him for his gallantry and said we'd prefer to wait for the late night bus. The last we saw of him was stuffing his trousers into his socks as he mounted the bike and rode wobbling into the night. He even saluted to us over his shoulder as he departed from sight.

We witnessed great nights at the 'Galty.' I recall the night we tried to get in to see Big Tom. The crowds were massive, four deep and while we managed to get as far as the ticket desk where we paid our money, that was as far as we progressed. The audience was so jam-packed inside we couldn't get past the foyer. I said we'd try the Banba instead.

At the ticket desk they refused to return our money until I explained that I would call the police as the 'Galty' that night was a safety hazard and that if a fire broke out no one was going to get out alive. We quickly got our refund after that.

I first met Tim when I was 18, that night in the Céilí section. We went out on and off for a good while and we finally got married when I was 26. Even then he was recognised to be a master craftsman, always in great demand. The money was good. One night early on in our relationship he offered my sister and myself a lift home in his car. As we walked out onto the Broadway, he linked us both and said he was parked a good bit down the road. However, he warned us, we might have to push start it as the car was a bit of a banger. My sister caught my eye and frowned, memories of the pushbike incident still fresh in her mind.

The car he stopped at and opened with his key was brand new, a Cortina.

It had red leather seats and round lights at the back, the latest top-of-the-range model at the time. It was so unusual for an Irish lad to own a new car in those days that we were speechless for the first mile or so. I can still recall the rich aroma of leather and that great new car smell. We went out steady after that.

The Galtymore was a home from home for so many of us during the 60s and in the decades following. It was so sad to read that the place finally closed down. I understand it's now a hole in the ground. The famous ballroom is no more but in our hearts and heads the memories live on as does Tim's mark on the landscape of London.

If you walk the streets of London some day, make sure to look down. Chances are you might be walking on my husband's paving and on the dreams of yesteryear, a time when we were young, carefree and everything seemed possible.

Máire Ní Gioblain lived and worked for most of her life in London. She is now retired and lives in County Galway.

As I was making my way to the Carlow road hitching spot, a large black Mercedes pulled up. The driver rolled his window down and asked if I wanted a lift. The said driver, I should say, I recognised immediately as Brendan Bowyer.

7

Thumbs Up For A Star

John O'Brien

I STARTED secondary school in Naas, Co. Kildare in 1965 in what was known as 'The Tech'. There was no bus service in my area in the countryside, which was 12 miles south of Naas on the main Carlow/Dublin road.

The only option at the time was to 'hitch' or as we called it 'thumb a lift.' My thinking at the time was that if someone was kind enough to stop for me, I would take the lift from them even if they were only going a mile or two. With this method, I was late on many occasions for school and, more importantly, dinner in the evenings on my way home.

On one particular day, I had managed to get as far as Kilcullen, which meant that I had another five miles to go. Kilcullen had one main road to Naas and Dublin, but was divided into two main roads heading south: one road to Carlow/Waterford and the other to Athy/Castlecomer/Kilkenny.

As I was making my way to the Carlow road hitching spot, a large black Mercedes pulled up. The driver rolled his window down and asked if I wanted a lift. The said driver, I should say, I recognised immediately as Brendan Bowyer.

I was stunned and speechless, but did manage to stutter a 'yes' before sitting in the front seat. Brendan, to his eternal credit, chatted away about school without mentioning who he was, though he must have been aware I recognised him.

A million thoughts went through my head during that five mile journey but I was only able to answer with a 'yes' or 'no' to his queries.

When we reached my stop, I mustered up enough courage to ask him for his autograph. He said he would be delighted, even if he had to wait while I scrambled through my schoolbag for a pen and bit of paper.

Patiently Brendan said: "Don't worry, I have something in the glovebox that might do." He reached over and pulled out a photograph of the Royal Showband and signed his name on the photo, saying: "I hope this will do the job?"

Such was my excitement that I just about got a "thank you so much" out. As he waved goodbye, his parting words were: "Sure, I might see you again sometime at a dance around here."

Remembering our chat, what stands out was the way he took an interest in what I was doing without talking about himself. A true gentleman. I couldn't wait to get home with the prized possession of his signed autograph in my hand. I ran down the laneway to our house as quickly as Ronnie Delany could at the time. I had two older brothers of dance-going age and one younger than me and I knew they would be excited to hear all about my encounter.

My father wasn't too up to date with the music scene but asked: "Is that the fella from Waterford who moves around on the stage trying to remove his jacket without opening the buttons?" – referring to the Hucklebuck moves.

"No," I answered. "That's Houdini you're thinking of."

In the innocence of the time, word spread around the locality to the extent that I became very popular with older girls, some of whom hadn't recognised my existence before then.

Alas, it wasn't me they wanted to kiss but Brendan's autograph and the photos of the other band members on the card I brought everywhere with me.

Needless to say, I couldn't wait to go to my first dance. My brother sneaked me in on St. Stephen's night to the Dreamland Ballroom in Athy. I was 14 years and 9 months old, still wet behind the ears and some turf mould in them, but I felt like a man ready to conquer and embrace the showband world.

I stood at the stage for the entire night, gazing in amazement at the band. Yes, I was totally starstruck watching 'my friend' Brendan Bowyer, the lead singer with the Royal Showband.

John O'Brien is a native of Ballymount, Co Kildare. Married with four children, his hobbies include walking, cycling and supporting Kildare GAA.

8

'Flower Power' In Callan

Joe Kearney

T HERE are many things I can never remember, the distance to the
moon, the speed of light, the speed of sound. So I shouldn't have been
surprised when the old song sprang out at me from the radio-speaker and
caught me unawares and unprotected. I stood entranced as memories
ran before me like the shadows that tried to escape from us on that night
in late-summer, so long, long ago.

"If you're going to San Francisco be sure to wear some flowers in your
hair..." Behind our shoulders a full harvest moon spotlit our ragged
progress. The hedgerows we passed between knew what we knew;
summer was in its death throes. Already the first whiffs of putrefaction
were leaking into this sharp night; the frail breath of a newly-born
autumn replacing the last rasping rattles of summer. Soon the return to
school would curtail our all-too-brief freedom. We were conscious that
in another part of the world the "Summer of Love" was coming to a close
but there it would be replaced by a glorious fall where the music and love
and life would continue, unlike the prospects that loomed ahead of
ourselves.

Tonight would be different, however, because Spider, Paulie, my best
friend Scully, his sister Kate and myself were going to bring "Flower
Power" to Callan, to the dance in the Parochial Hall, Green Street.

Moonlight was weakly reflected heavenward by the relic of summer's
garden; by a defiance of white convolvulus trumpets, mock funeral lilies
of the hedgerow. Perhaps that was why we chose to twine them into our
lengthened hair; the treasured locks that would soon be shorn in
preparation for classroom confinement.

We knew that we needed to look the part for the night ahead, that we
needed a uniform to single us out as being different from the assemblage
we would find in the hall; one that would mark us out for the mission ahead.
We had, after all, studied the pictures in FAB 208: Scott McKenzie with
turned-in shirt collars and flapping unbuttoned cuffs. The bell-ends of our

flared jeans had been frayed earlier and in true hippie spirit, we had hidden our shoes in a ditch and proceeded towards the town barefoot, wincing as we tried to ignore the bruises on our uncalloused soles. The cockles that we sported to proclaim our pilgrimage were the beads we borrowed from Kate, Scully's sister. Spider had donned a suit waistcoat three sizes too large and Kate was just herself, Scully's sister, one of the lads... almost.

Buttressed-up by the sweet sherry that Paulie had removed from the back of the press in his parlour and our breaths camouflaged by the clove drops carried resourcefully in Kate's handbag, we chanted out a throaty chorus into this velvet night when we would bring flowers, love and light to Callan.

Outside the hall, the Saturday night pulsed with escaping drumbeats and brassy horns; raw energy and promise of something else, something we dreamed of as musky, rich, vital, exciting. We pooled and counted out our cash, as scant in the upturned innocence of our palms as the sum total of our collective experience of love and stepped up to the door with its poster proclaiming: 'Playing tonight – Frankie McBride and the Polka Dots – Admission 7/6. Nine till One – Refreshments available at mineral bar in hall. No pass-outs.'

Planted in the foyer in a fog of cigarette smoke and as imposing as the back wall of a handball alley, we encountered the broad presence of Seamus Scanlon, on duty behind the table that had been earlier set up to serve as a ticket counter. His porcine pupils widened at the sight before him and then quickly reverted to their guarded norm as he swallowed a snigger into the folds of his neck. Important in pioneer-pin and kipper-tie that was as wide as the grin about his mouth, he greeted the motley crew: "How-ya Kate ... and the lads? Gran' night."

He then directed himself to Spider as he doled out a tongueful of buff tickets. "Did you notice Spider if there was a full moon when ye were comin' in?"

Spider, always one to trip on the wire in the minefield of parochial jibe, confirmed indeed yes, now that he came to think of it, there was a full moon. "I thought as much when I clocked the gimp of ye slingin' in the door," smirked Seamus, as he almost choked himself on the self-constructed gallows of wit.

The emotion stretched the bellyband of his pants to alarming limits of tolerance below the kippered tail of the tie. Recovering himself somewhat he shouted above the rock n' roll seeping out from under and around the door as Frankie spurred on the sweating jivers to "Go, go, go, go, Johnny, go, go, go".

"Oh by the way Spider, your timing is perfect," he shouted, as he nodded to the flower behind Spider's ear and the beads slung around his neck, "You're just in time for the ladies excuse-me".

"F...k off you fat b...x" was all Spider could struggle to say as he attempted to recover some dignity by bullying his way through the door and into the swelter of dancers.

It was all downhill from there on; no one would dance with us, not even the girls we knew as neighbours and friends. We were outsiders, contaminated by God knows what. Our confidence wilted as fast as the flowers in our hair. Kate got a few duty dances but soon, guiltily, joined us in our huddled sulk at the end of the hall. All that was left for us to do was jeer at the band and dancers alike. Sunburnt farmers sons and daughters, drapers assistants, bank clerks all drifted past in the sea of rhythmic waves, the gravitational tide which was controlled by the sweating bulk of cowboy-shirted Frankie. Round and round the hall they went, anti-clockwise in tweed jackets, drip-dry nylon shirts, corduroys, floral-patterned mini-skirts, pastel cardigans, high heels, spray-on hair-dos.

This was not our music; this was not our scene. We wanted Lovin' Spoonful, Mamas and Papas, Simon and Garfunkel, Bob Dylan, and what we got instead? We had Frankie McBride.

When Paulie became involved in a shoving match with some of the Slattery brothers in the gents toilets we knew it was time to leave. We would not be bringing San Francisco's lovin' to Callan tonight. We might as well go home.

The jingle of change in the back pocket of my jeans was equal to the price of two bags of chips. It was our sole consolation, and so we queued at the flap of Chuck's Wagon parked across the street from the hall.

I was just about to season the steaming mound of deep-fried spuds with the drum of salt when I heard Kate scream out behind me. As Frankie slipped into a little Buck Owens number, "I've got a tiger by the tale ..." I saw the Slatterys as shadowy silhouettes dancing about the fallen forms of three lads. They looked like some macabre mimicry of girls dancing around handbags except this was serious, dangerous. Scully, Paulie and Spider had been jumped upon when my back was turned. They curled together, lying in the street, where they circled, trampled, kicked: no excuse-mes here.

Distantly a car twisted up Bridge Street, through the Cross and eventually lit the top of Green Street and the Parochial Hall; by then it was over. The Slatterys were safely back at the dance, slipping past the kippered sentry. The lads limped behind the safety curtain of darkness that was the Fair Green so as to hide out until the coast was clear.

Kate and I walked away from the town numbed by what we had witnessed each with a bag of unsalted chips, cooling in our hands. Behind us Frankie was distantly pleading with us to: "put your sweet lips to the phone..." Then another sound, far less gentle, came sweeping through the music and into our consciousness. It was coming in our direction, from the town, the sound of the Slatterys Ford Zephyr, the unmistakeable miss-firing stutter of its six cylinders rapidly approaching.

"Quick," urged Kate and she pulled me beneath the shelter of an ash tree. "Pretend we're a courting couple."

Wrapped in a disguising embrace we were washed over by a probing rinse of bright headlights. Buried in one another's hair we listened to the big car slow down and heard some obscenity shouted in our direction. Then with a rev of frustrated anger they were suddenly gone, the lights stabbing sharp fingers into the dark hedges: the motor labouring onwards in its mission of unfinished business.

Safe once more, our racing pulses should have slowed down but strangely they refused to do so; instead the valves in the twin carburettors of our hearts continued to flutter as before, and we discovered that we were reluctant to break from the shelter of the embrace.

Maybe it was the fright or the convolvulus in Kate's hair; perhaps even the flakes of moonlight that speckled through the boughs of the ash trees and fell about her face like the lights from the glitter-ball suspended above the dance floor. They lay about us like a handful of silver coins cast generously down from the heavens. I don't know, but whatever it was on that night of late summer as a distant snare drum rattled out the finale of the Soldiers' Song, Kate ceased to be just Scully's sister and joined me in stepping across the threshold into another realm, into a beautiful enchanted place. It might be late in the season but at last the "Summer of Love" had found us.

Dr. Joe Kearney is a native of Callan, Co Kilkenny. A retired executive in the oil industry, he is also an award-winning documentary maker for RTÉ and has written for a number of published collections.

There was an interval break and this lady came up to me praising our performance and saying how much she enjoyed the music. She then asked if we were available to play at an Orange Hall dance also in Banbridge?

9

Lucky Escape On Night Of 'Miami Massacre'

Eddie Marmion

THERE is something unique about borders. That crease on a map that divides one community from another. And then there is the notion of a border crossing, the place where you hold your breath traversing no-man's-land. That's how we felt the night we fulfilled a commitment and performed a gig at the Kildress Inn in Cookstown, Co Tyrone.

I often thought about the name afterwards – Kildress. Oh, there's no doubt but we ourselves were dressed to kill that night. We were the Country Sounds Showband and I doubled on drums and vocals. I sometimes dig out an old photo or fan pic from the time and wonder at the youthful cut of us, shoulder length hair, hipsters, wide belts and medallions and chains around our necks. Your arse would be black and blue from young ones pinching you after a gig. We travelled wherever the work took us, north or south made no difference. In the early to mid 60s you could hardly keep up with the demands. There were four of us in the band, crammed into a battered Ford Transit. As sure as God, we must have carried a ton of gear in the back of that old workhorse.

We kept the repertoire varied, Rock 'n Roll, Country and a bit of Dixieland thrown in for good measure. We had a manager who sometimes came to the gigs. He was there the night we played a British Legion Club in Lisburn. We were careful in our music selection that night, conscious that a portrait of the Queen looked down upon the bandstand and that we were providing the music for a mainly Loyalist audience. No Sean South Of Garryowen, no Lonely Woods of Upton and definitely no Four Green Fields. There was an interval break and this lady came up to me praising our performance and saying how much she enjoyed the music. She then asked if we were available to play at an Orange Hall dance also in Banbridge.

I panicked. Said I'd have to talk to our manager but that we'd love to if we were available. I saw the same buck necking a mineral across the far side of the hall and made my way over to him. "I don't care if we have to sit at home watching The Late, Late Show, just tell her we are booked solid for the foreseeable future and that we can't do that Orange Hall gig."

When the dance finished and we were packing up he said: "I got you out of that one, Eddie, but I have a venue for you instead, the Kildress Inn in Cookstown." And that's how we came to play the hall that infamous night.

By the mid-seventies, the so-called Troubles had intensified in Northern Ireland. The old Transit was holding up but you had to fight the gears if you wanted to get any traction with the weight of the gear and the passengers. On the night in question the hall was full and we finished up at about 1.00 am with a rendition of 'The Queen'. We were anxious to get home and fairly threw in the gear to the back of the Transit.

Now, the road out of Cookstown was pretty desolate in those days. Out of nowhere we were overtaken by another, more up-to-date van. The driver slowed in front of us, trying to get us to stop. I was driving and decided it would be more prudent to drive on. Everyone was on high alert. I cranked up the gears and headed for the border. I could see in the rearview mirror the other van catching up again. It passed us and this time blocked the road ahead. We stopped. All the band members hopped out and walked towards the other driver.

"Jaysus boys," he said, laughing at us. "I've been trying to alert you that your back door is open and you're losing the drum kit along the road."

He was a member of another band that was also making their way back to the border. I often think of that night on the lonely road from the Kildress Inn in Cookstown. I particularly think on the July of each year for the past 42 years. On July 31, 1975, three members of the Miami Showband were killed as they returned from playing a gig in the Castle ballroom in Banbridge County Down.

Near the junction with Buskhill Road, they were flagged down by armed men dressed in British Army uniforms waving a red torch in a circular motion. During 'The Troubles' it was normal for the British Army to set up checkpoints at any time.

Thinking it was a legitimate checkpoint, they pulled in at the lay-by.

They were ordered to step from the minibus and stand facing the ditch with their hands on their heads.

At least four of the gunmen who manned the ambush were UDR soldiers, the locally recruited infantry regiment of the British Army in the North. It is suggested that at least five serving UDR soldiers were present at the checkpoint. All the gunmen were members of the UVF's Mid-Ulster Brigade, and had been lying in wait.

Out of sight of the band members, two of the gunmen placed a ten-pound time bomb in the rear of the minibus. The UVF's plan was to explode the bomb as the minibus reached Newry, killing all on board. There are some who believe that the reason the UVF decided to target the Miami Showband was because Nationalists held them in high regard; to attack the band was to strike the nationalists indirectly.

When the two gunmen closed the rear door, clumsy soldering on the clock used as a timer caused the device to explode prematurely, blowing the minibus apart and killing two of the "soldiers." From the Miami, Brian McCoy was the first to die, having been hit in the back by nine rounds from a 9mm pistol in the initial volley of gunfire. Fran O'Toole attempted to run away, but was chased down and machine-gunned 22 times, mostly in the face, as he lay supine on the ground.

Tony Geraghty also attempted to escape; but he was caught by the gunmen and shot at least four times in the back of the head and back. Both men had pleaded for their lives before they were shot; one had cried out: "Please don't shoot me, don't kill me."

Bassist Stephen Travers was seriously wounded by the shooting but survived by pretending he was dead as he lay beside the body of Brian McCoy.

Saxophone player Des McAlea was hit by the minibus's door when it was blown off in the explosion, but was not badly wounded. He lay hidden in thick undergrowth, undetected by the gunmen. He also survived.

However, the flames from the burning hedge (which had been set on fire by the explosion) soon came dangerously close to where he lay; he was forced to leave his hiding spot. Fortunately by then the gunmen had left the scene.

Lately I was driving and listening to a country station on local radio.

The DJ played Fran on lead vocals with the Miami singing a cover version of the Temptations great hit 'My Girl' and must confess that my eyes were blinded with tears.

Mine is not just sorrow for the murder of fine musicians and friends but a thing the psychologists call "survivor guilt."

You see we too played a gig in Banbridge that night, July 31, 1975. We played 'The First And Last Club' the night the Miami were playing 'The Castle Ballroom.' Our dance ended one hour before the Miami's did and we hit the road home earlier than them.

We travelled the same route that they took one hour later. When we passed the Buskhill junction, the rogue checkpoint had yet to be set up. It would be the next morning before we'd learn of the tragedy we so narrowly missed.

After the 'Miami Massacre' it took us a long time to get the courage to play north of the border. But we did return to the circuit eventually. You go wherever there is work, but somehow it was never the same.

May the Lord have mercy on all their sweet souls. They have been taken from us but no one will ever kill the music.

Eddie Marmion is a musician and storyteller from the Cooley Peninsula in County Louth. He has been employed for most of his life in the whiskey industry and is currently working with Teeling Distillery. Eddie has made multiple musical recordings and performs a Joe Dolan tribute act.

10

From The Listening Wall
To The Dance Hall

Eileen Casey

IT was the seventies and I was a teenager, mad for dancing and music. At that time, my father worked as a night telephonist, then he'd deliver the morning post. As a result of his job, he slept most afternoons and we'd have to be quiet as mice and creep around on tip-toe. However, no sooner would he have cycled off to work than out came the sewing machine, on went the record player and it was open house.

Mother bought a Singer sewing machine in 1957 and while the showband craze was full pelt (throughout the 60s and 70s mainly), her skills supplemented the family income. Girls I'd gone to school with, now working in Dubarry's Shoe Factory or The Moquette Factory (two thriving employers then), came for dress fittings. There was no such thing as appointments. Whoever called to the door was admitted...and fitted.

These young women were also dance-mad. The showband scene was alive and bucking (or Hucklebucking, I should say). Our Midlands town had a hall big enough for the weekly throng who came from miles around. Consequently, glamorous frocks had to be run up on a regular basis, modelled from remnants bought cheaply in drapery shops. Mother would be shown a style spotted in a popular magazine and she'd do her best to copy it, cutting out a pattern from old newspaper. These commissions would usually have a full skirt so there'd be plenty of 'swing' room and adequate space under the arms so there'd be no restrictions when it came to 'throwing shapes.'

Mother's favourite music then was Country & Western. Some evenings Big Tom's 'Four Roads To Glenamaddy,' was played to the point of needle fatigue but Larry Cunningham's 'Don't Let Me Cross Over,' was also a contender. Ray Lynam and The Hillbillies and Sean Dunphy were popular too. She'd often hum 'The Old Refrain,' as she steered her material through the machine.

When she liked a record very much, she'd set the player up so that it played over and over. One of my older sisters would intervene with rock n' roll as an antidote from her overload. Brendan Bowyer and The Big Eight was a favourite and even though The Hucklebuck was a few years earlier (1965), it was still on the playlist. Joe Dolan's 'Good Looking Woman,' was guaranteed to activate the jiving cells, which is exactly what happened at fittings. When mother finished pinning the tucking, it was 'jive time.'

I'd grab whoever it was being decked out and we'd both quickstep out of the parlour where mother kept her machine (this room was also my parent's bedroom). In the tiny hallway, we'd gyrate, our bodies twitching with rhythm. There was a lot of laughter too. We were young and healthy and music was all we could ask for.

I was still in secondary school and mother wouldn't hear of me going to proper dances until I was 16, just like my three sisters before me. To help me over the transitional timeframe, she'd walk down with me to the Marian Hall some Fridays and we'd sit on the low wall surrounding it, hearing the showbands belt out their hits. We'd go mostly when the weather was mild and the evenings bright. She'd have a bag of bulls-eyes or clove drops in her pocket and we'd munch away, swaying to the music. I'd dream about going to a proper dance. In the dream, I'd imagine myself being whisked onto the floor by a succession of handsome partners. And of course, overhead was the glitteriest glitter ball that ever existed. Two of my sisters were working in Dublin in the civil service. Another was training to be a nurse in London. She'd go to the Hammersmith Palais most weeks but the two in Dublin had The Ierne and The Irish Club. However, on the weekends when they'd come home, I'd hang around them while they got ready for the Friday trip to the dancehall. Roly Daniels, Brendan O'Brien and Red Hurley were just some of the fabulous singers that we each hummed and spun to in that small bedroom under the eaves. If a match had been lit the whole place would have combusted with all the hair lacquer and deodorant sprayed.

When they'd gone to the dance, I'd wait patiently for their return, living each note and each movement with them when they came home. If by chance, I'd gone down with mother to our 'listening wall', I was able to name the songs I'd heard and they'd tell me if they'd been dancing to it and with whom. It made the experience more real and alive.

And then, miraculously I was 16 and it was my turn to shine. For the big occasion, my sisters came down from Dublin with a new sleeveless dress and matching jacket, silky seamed nylons, make up and perfume. There was also a new pair of pointy-toed shoes with high heels. I remember the dress well. It had tiny pink roses on it and a white collar. It didn't seem at all odd that I wouldn't be wearing a dress made by my mother. Although she'd often made dresses for me, on this occasion I was treated to a shop bought outfit. One of my sisters tied my hair up with pink bobbles and the other put make up on me, my first time to wear it. Blue eye-shadow and mascara set off a light dusting of face powder. My lipstick was a bright colour and shiny but it tasted strange, like plastic, and I worried that it might stain my teeth. While I was being prepared for dancehall bliss, I was bombarded with the 'dos' and 'don'ts' of dancehall etiquette.

I was never to refuse a boy's request to dance (I never have and never would either). I was to be careful with the slower dances and not allow any liberties. My partner's hand could travel no lower than mid-way down my back and I was to resist any efforts to be pulled into a tight embrace. On no account was I to accept the offer of an orange or lemonade. On the face of it, having a mineral with a boy seemed innocent enough but they assured me that it had deeper significance attached to it. That if I were to go for the mineral, it meant the boy had another agenda. Mother had already advised me about these subtleties.

When I was completely 'done up,' I stood on the fitting chair in the parlour-cum-bedroom and looked at myself meticulously in the mirror over the small fireplace that every room in that council house had. I saw the backs of my legs, noting the seams of my stockings were straight. I saw that the dress came to just above my knees and when I stepped down and looked at my face and hair, I could hardly credit it was me. I thought my sister had been a little heavy-handed with the make up but she'd assured me that by the end of the night, it would be well worn off.

As it happened, my first dance experience was in a giant marquee, erected because there was a festival on. It was late autumn and the weather had turned cold. Hugo Duncan and The Tall Men were playing. We set off, the 'Three Musketeers' mother christened us. She stood at the gate waving, watching us all the way down the street.

It had rained torrentially for about five days and nights and the soles of my new shoes had no grip at all. When we got to the field where the marquee was, planks of wood had been laid down to walk on because the ground was so muddy. The place was thick with people queuing to get in and we could hear the support band strike up a lively tune. We joined the queue, jostled along by the banter of the crowd. Some of them were impatient to get dancing. When the support band launched into 'Good Looking Woman,' the strain proved too much. Impromptu jiving partnerships sprung up, movement which unsettled my position on the already slippery plank of wood. I tried to clutch onto my sister's coat but before I knew what was happening, I had fallen into the mud. Very squelchy mud too. I could feel it seeping through my finery; it had even splashed onto my hair and one side of my face.

We returned home, three very dejected Musketeers. Although my sisters were disappointed at missing the dance, they rallied around with mother to restore me to cleanliness and good cheer.

Water was heated; a quick wash ensued followed by a delicious hot cup of cocoa. There would be many another night, mother said, and she was right. There was.

Eileen Casey is originally from the midlands and now lives in Dublin where she is a creative writing tutor. She has had several poems and stories published in periodicals and books.

Minor Miracle
In The Early Hours

Ed Cunningham

I'VE had people curse me in my time but I'll never forget the torrent unleashed in my direction by seven other occupants of our old Morris Minor around half three on a mid-July morning as we returned from a dance in the early seventies.

I was driving faithful old Herbie (ELI 711). There was a full house that night, that is eight of us aboard.

Now, I had long been of the opinion, after several close shaves, that when Herbie registered 'Empty' on the dashboard with the yellow light permanently on, there was still plenty of petrol in reserve.

It was said I had driven it on mere fumes most of its life. I knew Herbie would never let me down. Well, I thought I knew.

Because I didn't drink, I got to drive our cousins' cream Morris 1100 to dances too (I was a designated driver before anyone heard of the term). Theirs was a lovely car and was spoilt by being kept at least half-full of fuel most of the time.

Herbie, in contrast, got 10 shillings worth from Johnny Hanamy's pump in Church St, Clara, Offaly on its birthday to swell its tank capacity past the quarter-full mark once a year. The rest of the time it hovered between empty and almost empty.

Between it and the cousins' car I got to drive a gang of us to dances all across the midlands for a few memorable summers.

Otherwise I would never have been able to afford or attend the musical milieus of the late sixties/early seventies when Joe Dolan, Brendan Bowyer, Thin Lizzy and their ilk adorned our ballroom stages and marquees until the early hours.

We (the brother and I) had no money as such. And going to dances was an expensive business. Getting into the hall or marquee cost 10 shillings, maybe 12s/6d (a sizeable sum, especially in my late father's estimation).

Then there could be chips and Club Oranges to be purchased if you hit it off with a young lady. And a packet of Major (cigarettes in case any of you think I'm referring to anything else).

So we worked out a system. We'd chip in for a ticket between two or three of us which would be exchanged (as a Pass Out) every hour. I'd wait in the car while the brother, for example, tried his luck for an hour. Then he'd get a Pass Out ticket, give it to me and while he stayed in the car I'd 'dance'. It certainly concentrated the mind when the clock was ticking and the night was disappearing.

Anyway, on the July morning that those curses were to rain down on my head, we were seriously out 'foreign' – Birr, I think.

Despite being laden to the gills with passengers, Herbie didn't complain. What a great old servant.

It was a pearlescent night, one of those I sensed the world held its breath at the peak of summer each year before reluctantly yielding to the inevitable, initially imperceptible, slip into autumn and thoughts of the narrowing gap to returning to school or college.

We were tipping across the Boora Bog road, here and there hidden by the light dusk mists that hovered over the brown lunar-like landscape under a faded full moon.

A few of us were in triumphant mood. Some decent girl had charitably participated in a few kisses and cuddles at the back of the hall after agreeing to dance and take up the offer of a Club Orange.

It was so innocent: the romance of it all, the thrill of the chase and the ego-boost of acceptance would stretch across the following week, sustaining emotional well-being until new conquests were boldly sought and courted at the next dance.

Some of us were not in such good form. All attempts to chat and impress several females in the course of the night had failed abysmally, prompting waves of adolescent self-doubt – and merciless ribbing from those who had 'squared'. But, hey, there was always hope at the next outing. Hope sprang eternal in those young hearts.

For most of us at that stage of the return journey just a few hours of slumber beckoned before the cows had to be milked and the grinding routine of subsistence farming ensnared our bodies, if not our minds, for another while.

Despite the intensely cramped conditions in the car some of my passengers had already yielded to the circadian rhythms of such a late hour when Herbie fired a first warning.

I felt the jiggle halfway along that lengthy, straight stretch of road. We were, to all intents and purposes in the middle of nowhere (no offence to locals but evidence of life at that hour back then was non-existent).

I timidly, presciently perhaps, asked those still half awake how many miles they reckoned we still had to cover.

Before they could settle on an estimate, Herbie emitted a near-humanlike belch. The impossible was no longer possible. It had tried manfully to sniff the last stain of petrol from the remotest region of the tank before chugging to a halt with what sounded like an exasperated gasp.

We were stranded, miles and miles from anywhere, in the middle of the bog. And it was half-three in the morning. There were no all-night petrol stations then; no mobile phones. And not a house in sight. We might as well have been on the moon.

If I were to replicate the curses that ensued and the threats of grievous bodily harm that accompanied them, the following pages would turn crimson. Suffice to say that the 'curse of the seven snotty orphans' on me sounded like a benign blessing compared with the vitriolic vicissitudes wished upon my person for the rest of my about-to-be-shortened life.

We were looking at a possible two-hour walk. And I'd be hounded all the way for being a miserly so-and-so who wouldn't put a few bob's worth of petrol in the car and they after buying me chips and giving me cigarettes because I was broke.

It must have seemed an odd scenario to the man in the car who appeared out of nowhere from the mists of the hollow stretch of road ahead.

If I were in his boots, I'd have kept going. I would not have felt safe letting down the window to a jostling gaggle of long-haired, bad-tempered youths arguing on the side of the road at that hour of the morning.

But stop he did.

And he didn't stop at that.

Miraculously, he produced a gallon can of petrol from the boot.

He said he had been in the same boat once and never left home without backup since. We profusely thanked him (and God I think) for his miraculous intervention,

He not alone replenished Herbie's tank, he refused steadfastly to take a penny for the fuel. He was an angel of mercy, a true knight of the road. We never got his name but we never forgot his deed.

That Good Samaritan taught us a lesson which we in turn passed on by coming to the aid of others in similar exigencies when, maybe previously, we might not have done so.

More importantly, he saved me from being banished as the designated driver – on the promise that we'd never leave for a dance again without a can in the boot.

And we didn't. I made sure of that though I'd be lying if I told you there was always petrol in it.

Eddie Cunningham is an author and journalist whose fascination with cars has seen him become an expert in the field with Independent Newspapers for quarter of a century. A father of four grown-up daughters, the Co Offaly native is a former deputy editor of the 'Irish Independent' and is a keen creative writer.

A Royal Dilemma
On The Glenshane Pass

Pat Larkin

THE first band I ever saw live was the Royal Showband. When they came on stage I was blown away by the sound. It was so powerful with all the brass instruments. Brendan Bowyer, Tom Dunphy, Charlie Mathews and Jim Conlon all performed songs on that night. The Ulster Hall was jam-packed with around 4,000 people. From then on I was a fan.

As a teenager growing up in Belfast in the sixties, Friday was always a great day. That was when the New Musical Express and the Spotlight magazine came into the shops. The Friday I'm telling you about was no different to the others. I rushed home from work, had a swift wash, a splash of Brut aftershave and donned my mohair suit. In the mirror I looked the part. With my NME and Spotlight in hand I met up with my friends for a few pints at our local bar, the Glenowen.

Brian Kerr (Herbie), Joseph McCrory (Josie), were similarly dressed to kill. After some chat we got down to business; where were we going later. Usually we'd go into Belfast to a dance in Romano's, The Starlight or the local Cabaret Club. However this Friday was changed thanks to Spotlight Magazine. We saw an advert for the Fiesta Ballroom in Letterkenny, announcing that The Royal was playing there that night.

It started out as a laugh. But as the cogs started to turn we considered really how long would it take us to get there? Who's driving? The joking was turning into a plan of action. I'd just bought my first car, it was a Standard 10 (Super) costing £35.

We worked out that Letterkenny was 100 miles away. If we left at 7.30pm we could arrive at 10.30pm. The dance started at 11pm, the Royal on stage from 12-2.00am. There were bound to be lots of talent there (girls) who would love to meet good-looking guys from Belfast. We drank, got 10-bob's worth of petrol and set off. This was in the 60s, so we had to go through all the small towns Antrim, Randalstown, Toomebridge could throw at us.

Things were going well, plenty of craic in the car as we coasted along at about 45mph. Then I noticed that we were losing power and had to change down gear. A few minutes later I had to change down another gear and was really getting worried. It was pitch dark outside and I didn't fancy breaking down in the middle of nowhere.

Herbie asked if my boot was to the floor? I said 'yes.' From the rear seat, Josie shouted: "Hey boys look behind you." All we could see were the lights away below us in the distance. We'd been climbing up the Glenshane pass and the wee car was doing its best on such a massive steep hill. When we eventually got to the top it took off like a rocket and we were back on course.

We reached Letterkenny around half 10 and stopped at Peadar's Bar which had two petrol pumps outside to get another ten-bob's worth. As I was filling the petrol, this big Mercedes pulled up and who was it but Tom Dunphy of the Royal. I shouted across: "Hi ya Tom, do you know where the dance hall is?" He pointed: "Down the road on the left hand side." I said "Thanks, we'll see you later."

With the car geared up for the journey home, we headed into Peadar's Bar. At around 11.30pm we made our way down to the Fiesta with enough time to check the talent before the Royal came on stage. The hall was jammed so we positioned ourselves near the stage to listen to Brendan belting out his hits.

Josie got itchy feet and wanted to line-up some girls. We spotted three likely candidates and politely asked: "Would you like to dance?"

"No thanks," all three responded. We decided they must be with their boyfriends so not to be put off we picked out another three – but got the same replies.

This was the theme for the night, nobody would dance with us. We returned to the front and watched the band until at 1.50am Tom Dunphy announced the last set of dances. To our surprise three girls came up and asked us out on the floor. Then the next song came and three different girls came over to ask us up. For the second last song, Bowyer sang "Love Thee Dearest" and the three girls we fancied most asked us up for this dance. That song over, we all applauded before he went straight into the Hucklebuck. The same three girls danced on and stood with us through the National Anthem.

The dance was over but the girls were still by our sides. We asked if they fancied a mineral, got six bottles of orange and headed to the stage for the handout pictures and autographs. We walked outside with the girls and we all managed to squeeze into the wee 10 for a lumber (kiss) – four in the back and me and this girl in the front. After about 15 minutes of what we would call 'cafuffling,' we exchanged addresses and waved them off on their bus.

It was 3.30am and by the time I got to Derry the two boys were fast asleep and I was fighting tiredness too. When we reached the Glenshane Pass it was covered in thick fog. Visibility was reduced to a yard and I shouted at the boys to wake up. Josie asked "are we in heaven?"

I said: "No we're in fog on the Pass." He got out and walked in front waving a lit cigarette as a signal. I followed this spark of light for about 10 minutes until the fog lifted enough so I could drive on normally.

It was 6.45am when we arrived home. The milkman was doing his rounds and we bought three lovely pints of cold milk from him.

It was as near perfect an end as we could imagine to a night chasing dreams on a 200-mile round trip.

Pat Larkin is a native of Belfast and now likes to spend his weekends at his residence in Kilmacrennan, Co Donegal. Married with two children, he is retired but still enjoys taking part in local music sessions.

| 13 |

Anthem For An Era...

Kathleen Finan

SOMEONE once declared that history was the collision of small moments before they grew into something momentous.

Little did I know when I had an accident in the hotel where I was working in Ireland that I was about to embark on a journey that would write a whole new chapter in my life's story. In fact, it changed the course of my life completely.

I had never contemplated going to England to work but my mother had booked to go over there to visit relatives when I suffered my fall.

Now mum and I were very, very close and she couldn't bear the thoughts of leaving me behind unable to fend properly for myself.

At the last minute she arranged for me to travel with her and before we knew it, we were in Kilburn, London at my sister's place.

My brother-in-law, Tommy Hurley, was a decent man and he took me out for a tour on the buses. When my mother asked me what I thought of London after I came back, I told her: "I'd never live around here."

Tommy was at his wits end to keep me occupied while we were visiting him and my sister, Mary. On one of my first nights in Kilburn, he wheedled one of his friends to accompany me to the Galtymore for a dance. It was a moment when the flapping of a butterfly's love wings would lead to a life-long romance.

The person he had organised to chaperone me was a stunning looking Irish fella who appeared before me with a mop of curly black hair. He was dressed in a thin grey suit and grey shoes. It was love at first sight. Michael initially didn't go down so well with my mother. She described him as "a bit of a teddy boy."

He took me out dancing for the fortnight I was there and I'd never have gone back only Mum insisted that I accompany her home.

Even when I arrived back I remained listless and couldn't wait to see Michael again. Soon after I told my mother that I had made up my mind that I was going.

"For what. For a 'Teddy boy'?" she queried.

I was about 25 at this time but was old enough to know what I wanted. Despite the fact that mum didn't talk to me for two weeks, even when I met her down the town, I wasn't for turning.

Life though isn't simply black and white. No sooner had I landed in England than the opposite happened – I was now pining for my mother. We had been inseparable up to then and every time a letter arrived from home, I was in floods of tears.

Michael put up with my antics for a while, hoping that I would settle down and get used to a new way of life.

Unfortunately, the feeling of missing my mother and home persisted, so I bawled my eyes out whenever the letters arrived. One night, exasperated at my behaviour, he snatched the letter out of my hand, tore it in two and said firmly: "The best thing for you to do is go back to Ireland."

I can tell you that ended my crying game pretty quickly. I came to my senses and after a while Mum did too.

She saw that Michael was a good man and she made sure she attended our wedding, wishing me and my 'Teddy boy' the best of luck on our big day.

By the time we got married, I had known Michael a few years but he had been living in England for up to 15 years. He had gone over with his sister Bridie. They were part of a family of four whose mother had died of a heart attack when she was only 22.

Michael's father had a serious drink problem from a young age and wanted to put the children in an orphanage but their granny and granddad took them in to their own home.

When they died, Michael was left the farm and whatever money that was there. He was something of an entrepreneur even at 15 years of age and with the few bob, he bought a van.

He ferried women who were expecting babies to and from hospitals. More lucratively, he used the van to bring people to dances – up to 15 could be shoe-horned in when the occasion demanded.

One night he was stopped by the guards and when the sergeant looked in the window, he asked him: 'How many have you in there, Michael."

"Fifteen and counting," replied Michael as the lawman waved him on. After years married in England, Michael and myself returned to

Ireland in 1971 and ended up in Roscommon with our four children – two boys and two girls.

We both have that night in the Galtymore to thank for our collision in life which has led to 54 years of marriage. Many years later we were down at Listowel Races and retired to the Devon Inn for a drink in the evening. When Michael went up to the bar, it was packed and he struck up a conversation with two men who were waiting to be served as well.

"Are you on your own," one of them asked?

"No," Michael responded. "I'm with a woman I met in the Galtymore many years ago."

'Begob," said the man, "my name is Pat Byrne and I owned the Galtymore.

And the other man added: "And I'm the man who knocked it down."

The story didn't finish there as Michael told them that our godson, Peter Burke, had the honour of playing the last disc in the Galtymore before it closed. There had been a grand finale night for the public but this one some time later was for all the people who had either worked or been part of it.

Peter wrote a special song about his mother and father, how they'd met and what they did for him. Somehow, the recording – which I still have – echoes what happened to thousands of Irish people exiled on the other island – including Michael and myself.

It was an anthem for an era that is no more.

Kathleen Finan is a native of Mallow, in Cork. She now lives in Roscommon town with her husband Michael. They have four grown-up children and the couple still love to go dancing.

Musical Echoes

James Walsh

SOMETIMES when its quiet I find that I am listening to my heartbeat. There is a musicality to its rhythm that fascinates me. I realise that there is music in my blood. I am proud to be part of a musical family – a dynasty – the Brose Walsh Band.

Our musical history spans the best part of 80 years and even some of the instruments we play have a personal history. You might think, if that saxophone could speak what would it say? But consider this, it does speak whenever one of us puts the old mouthpiece to our lips, and blows. Those sweet notes echo down the years.

My father and some fellow musicians started playing house dances around Belcarra, County Mayo, in the 1930s. The band was formally launched on Christmas night at the local Horseshoe Hall in Frenchill near Castlebar in 1938. They were becoming recognised locally and were asked to provide the musical entertainment at the cinema in Castlebar. The rule at the time was that the live part of the programme had to be of longer duration than the film itself. However disaster struck when a fire burnt down the cinema and the band's instruments were destroyed in the blaze. Local people held a benefit night at the military barracks so that the band might raise funds to replace the precious instruments. It was around this time that the saxophone was given to my father. It was donated by an uncle living in America, the same Martin tenor sax that we play today. From those early beginnings my father went on to form the famous Brose Walsh Band.

He built a dancehall in Belcarra in 1947 – The Arcadia Ballroom. Brose realised that Ireland was changing. Electricity was being rolled out across the nation. There was a new hunger for entertainment. Music from across the Atlantic and the Irish Sea was replacing the more staid dancehall and céilí sounds of previous times. You could plug in an amplifier, an electric guitar, kick over the music stand and know that the age of the showband had arrived. The dance audience wanted jive and

Rock n' Roll and the Brose Walsh Band was more than happy to rise to the occasion.

Through the 40s and 50s the band toured the country and built an immense following. The Connaught Telegraph of Saturday 8th October 1960 carried a two page spread trumpeting the commencement of the Brose Walsh Band's US tour. In that year we played across America and during our itinerary drummed up support amongst the Irish American community for the new Democratic presidential hopeful – John Fitzgerald Kennedy. We handed out JFK badges at all our dance engagements.

Back in Ireland the 1960s represented the high point in show band fever. By the end of that decade Brose had two bands on the road, the second was the Rockaways. In 1970 we played for the Nixons during their Irish visit. One day the postman delivered a letter to the family home that bore the embossed crest of the White House in Washington. It was a personal letter of thanks from Patricia Nixon, the First Lady. Photographs from the time show the lineup. There's my father, myself and my brothers Tomas and John Noel, all part of the ensemble. We have entertained dance-goers all over Ireland, Britain and the U.S. We were even there for some of the closing dances in the Galtymore Ballroom in Cricklewood, London

Over the years, from the heights of the bandstand we have seen much of humanity waltz past our feet. We have seen the good, the bad and the great. We have witnessed romance and joy, tears and tantrums. Gruelling travel often created pressure on family life, but we are blessed to have supportive wives and family. We believe that deciding to abstain from alcohol helped us greatly in surviving the demands of the music industry.

My father had a most mischievous sense of humour. One local character, an unmarried middle-aged man, once told Brose that he had exhausted the romantic possibilities in his own town and wished to widen the geographical net. He knew that we were regularly engaged to play the Ierne Ballroom in Dublin and expressed an interest in coming up there with us. We agreed, and our friend danced the night away with civil servants, teachers and nurses. On the way back home he told us that there was one girl in particular who caught his fancy – a nurse but that she was reluctant to give him more than one dance. My father counselled that faint heart never won a fair lady and suggested that he accompany the band back to the Ierne the following weekend. He did, but complained that the result was the same, one dance with Juliet and nothing more. That was when my father hatched his plan and decided to play Cupid. He told our romance starved Romeo to buy a light coloured jacket, as near to white as he could and to make sure to wear a tie and that we would take him courting to Dublin one more time. On the night in question midway through the dance, Brose stopped playing and in a very serious voice inquired if there was a doctor in the house. As was pre-arranged, our friend nimbly skipped up to the stage and Brose spoke urgently to him off mike. Romeo was ushered back stage and the music continued. Sometime later Brose made a further announcement. He thanked our 'doctor' for his prompt service and for averting a medical emergency. After the dance we loaded up the bus, had something to eat and were ready to drive the long trek homewards. There was no sign of our friend. We waited the best part of an hour and sure enough he came swaggering up Parnell Square, tie undone and the white jacket unbuttoned. How did he get on we asked?

"Mighty" he replied with a smile as broad as O'Connell Street, "Just mighty. The only pity is that I left it so late to join the medical profession."

The Brose Walsh Band is still going strong featuring myself, James, together with my brothers Tomas and John Noel. Sadly, Brose passed away in 1995 at the age of 75. However, nowadays we are proud to know that a third generation of the family is there to join us on stage. That 1940s Martin tenor saxophone is being played by my nephew, Alan.

Family history is still being written in musical notes.

James Walsh and his brothers still play with the Brose Walsh Band.
They want to thank all those who have supported them over the years,
who have given them such rich memories and so much fun.

The Night Bridie Gallagher Played Kilmainham Wood

Pat Cussen

IN the timespan of my youth, certain events occurred which act like signposts for my memory. Just like the oft-posed question: "Where were you when you heard John F Kennedy was shot?" I can ask and get my bearings from knowing where certain showbands played on certain dates back in that land of Tír na nÓg.

It is close to 60 years now since Bridie Gallagher sang in Kilmainham Wood in Co Meath but locals of a certain vintage anchor their recall of history by referring to that night. And there is good reason why it has lasted down the decades because for a small, rural community, Bridie's visit was a standout moment in their lives. She was booked to play in the marquee but such was her powers of attraction that not only was the venue crowded but the entire village was heaving with the number of visitors who turned up to hear her sing her hit songs.

Even now six decades later, it is why old people when they congregate often say: "By the way were you there the night Bridie Gallagher played in Kilmainham Wood?"

Not as many people were present – but those who were never forgot – the night Paddy Cole played Moynalty with his new band, The Capitol. Paddy had been a fixture with Maurice Lynch's band for years but the night he arrived in Moynalty, he hardly knew the lads in the new band and was hoping to bed himself in during the dance.

The trouble for him was that it was a night when the heavens opened up and to make matters even worse, there was a hole in the waterproof material directly above the bandstand area.

It must have been hard enough for Paddy to get his musical timing with new musicians around him but to keep singing in the rain as the night progressed showed his resilience, not to mention his professionalism and dedication, to give the punters value for money.

So if anyone ever asks you where were you when Paddy Cole joined the Capitol and got a right royal baptism into the bargain, you can tell them that for sure, you were in Moynalty that night.

Fewer people will be able to answer the next riddle – where were you the night the Melody Aces played the El Dorado in Oldcastle? Now they played the venue many times in their career but only once when the fog descended so thick that you couldn't see six inches beyond your nose.

The chances are most people will tell you they stayed at home because truth to tell, only lunatics like myself and my friends ventured out that particular evening.

This area is near Loughcrew and the fact that it is hilly means thick fog congregates around the area at nighttime.

Our gang though thought the sun and moon shone out of this group and there was no way we were going to be thwarted by a blanket fog.

So the driver of our car, who would later become my brother-in-law, declared that we could beat the elements if we got a volunteer to sit out on the bonnet for the journey to Oldcastle. The thinking was, the man outside would be a few yards ahead of the rest of us inside the car, and could pound a warning out on the bonnet if we were too close for comfort to a ditch or wall or an errant donkey grazing the long acre.

Eventually one of the group was inveigled to become that outside hero. It worked out well too as he got us to our destination without leaving the road – though from memory I don't think we came across another soul out or about that night. However when we arrived we were disappointed that there was no one there except ourselves and the band.

What should have been a night to forget turned into a night to remember as the lads in the Melody Aces asked us what songs we wanted to hear and then played them especially for us.

You can gather from that occasion that if anyone asks: 'Where were you when the Melody Aces played requests for everyone in the hall?" that there was only a handful of people who can answer it truthfully.

I will finish by highlighting the fun we had getting to and from dances. Part of the planning was to have your lift arranged in advance because cars were nowhere near as plentiful as they are now. Even with the forward planning, there were occasions when a Prefect or Anglia would be full and one or two people still hadn't a lift.

One resourceful driver came up with the idea that after the seats were filled front and back, he could squeeze two more people in if the lads inside wound down the windows to allow bodies in by lying straight across those already inside.

It was a loading operation that required plenty of dexterity and while we travelled with hardly enough room to breathe, it also meant that we all got to the dance.

I suppose it's always been part of the Irish psyche to have a bit of fun at someone else's expense. And so it came to pass that one night we decided to do that by taking part of the ignition out of an Anglia – very popular cars at the time – when the driver and the crew he had delivered to a dance had left the car park area.

After the dance we waited with baited breath for them to approach the car. Watching from a distance we were giddy as we anticipated the reaction of the driver and passengers to our mischief making.

Instead our jaws dropped as all eight piled into the vehicle, and the driver turned the engine over straight away before driving off into the night.

"How in God's name did he manage that," we asked one another, somewhat bewildered at what we had just witnessed.

Then it dawned on us – there were about a dozen Anglias in the same row and somehow we had mixed up the cars.

The joke was now on us and we had to go from vehicle to vehicle before finding one that was unlocked and which had part of its engine missing. Luckily, we managed to put the missing part back before the owner became any the wiser.

During those dancing days, different drivers would bring us to different venues across Meath, Cavan and sometimes during Lent as far as Dublin. One such driver was slightly eccentric in our eyes because not only would he drive us, he also used the time with a captive audience in his car to sing several songs he had in his repertoire. We were happy to listen to one or two but after that we felt less and less inclined to give him our full attention.

Occasionally some of the smart Alecs in the back seat would crack jokes at his expense or simply refuse to stay quiet during his attempted rendition of yet another song.

Peeved at the behaviour, he jammed on the brakes and ordered everyone out onto the side of the road despite our protestations of innocence. He then turned the car and went home alone.

You never knew what to expect on a night out back then, but tell me "Where were you on the night...?"

Pat Cussen is a native of Moynalty, Kells, Co Meath. He married Marian Cahill (RIP) and they had five children. A former salesman with Clover Meats, he is now retired and his hobbies include GAA and horseracing.

| 16 |

Avoiding An Ambush
At The GPO

Michael Walsh

I HAD a fanatical interest in the showband scene in the sixties and seventies. This new-found transition in the dancing world from orchestral-type music was like a breath of fresh air for a country lad looking for change not only in music, but in the way bands dressed and performed on stage.

The new era was coming alive with lots of new songs and sounds. Rock 'n roll was by this time accepted as a genre and no matter where you travelled, the showband scene was your greatest guarantee of enjoyment and meeting people.

I started to experience all of this back in Tipperary and kept it up when I moved to Dublin in my late teens. I introduced myself to the dancing meccas in the city – The National Ballroom, Olympic, Galway Arms, Ierne, Arcadia and many others which catered for the top bands. My favourite ballroom was the National in Parnell Square and it was here that I met the love of my life.

One Thursday night I'd been at a meeting on North Circular Road and decided afterwards to pop into the National where The Smokey Mountain Ramblers were playing. The night was exceptional. Dancing is a bit like golf, some days you are just in the mood for it and everything goes so well.

Towards the end of the night, I danced with a girl who told me she came from the Kingdom. Did that make her an angel, I wondered?

I was concentrating so much on my steps that I didn't get to ask her many questions until the end of the three encores. By that time, I must admit that I had stepped on her toes more than once but she didn't complain.

That was a good omen.

I assured my patient partner that usually I danced better than this. She said it was okay to make mistakes. She asked me where I came from and when I replied "Tipperary', she said she knew some nurses from there. I was pleased to hear that, as my fear always was of meeting someone who might be from a county at war with Tipperary such as Cork, Kilkenny or Wexford. In those days being from a prominent hurling county branded you in the eyes of someone from a rival camp and somewhat an enemy.

My partner explained that there was virtually no hurling in Kerry, adding that she had no interest in either hurling or football. That was great to hear. At the end of the night, a friend who happened to be sharing a house with my dancing partner said she had a "lift home." This was music to the ears of girls in those days as cash was scarce and anyone rattling the keys of a car had an advantage over someone on a Rudge bicycle, or walking.

So four of us packed into the Austin in Parnell Square and headed back towards the North Circular Road. The house we arrived at off Aughrim Street was shared by four girls, two Marys, Bernice and Maura whom I had just met. To my amazement, one of the Marys in question was someone I had met earlier in the evening at the meeting. I thought to myself that the omens were on my side.

The owner of the car which had got us to this house turned out to be a Johnny Cash fan and picking up a guitar owned by one of the girls he gave us soul-felt rendering versions of many Cash songs, including, 'I Walk the Line.'

As I walked back to my digs on the North Strand under a moon-lit sky humming some of Johnny's songs, I felt this could be the beginning of something special.

I arranged to meet her at the GPO in O'Connell Street the following Tuesday at 7.30 pm to go to a film. I got there at seven.

The tension was unbearable as it was common in those days to be 'stood up.' Panic set in as 7.25 ticked over on Clery's Clock across the road where many other hopefuls were also waiting. Many thoughts crossed my mind; she had missed the No. 10 bus; she mistook the time; she was delayed coming off nursing duty or the ultimate thought – she changed her mind.

Out of the blue, a young, pretty girl approached me just before half seven and asked me if my name was Anthony. I said no, that I was christened Michael, but some called me Joseph because that was my second name.

She looked me up and down saying I looked like the fella she had made a date with the previous week.

I wished her luck in finding her date. She lingered a little more and then clasped my hand, smiling as she said: "If your date doesn't show up, maybe we could take in a movie, or go for a few drinks."

I didn't know what to say. By now she was holding both my hands when who arrived with a puzzled look on her face but Maura – my date.

The other girl turned crimson before apologising to both of us about the case of mistaken identity. I was much happier that the girl I asked out was the one I would now go with to the pictures.

Within a year Maura and I were engaged and got married soon afterwards. We continued to attend dances and still do to this day but often wonder what would have happened if she had not shown up? But that's the great thing about Maura – she always had a great sense of timing – on and off the dance floor.

Michael Walsh is a native of Toomevara in Co Tipperary. He is co-compiler/editor and publisher of the book on Fr. Aedan McGrath: 'From Navan to China.' Living in Dublin with Maura, they have four children and eight grandchildren. Their main hobby in life remains dancing.

Sailing For Muff

Brendan Moran

M Y ship, a Royal Navy Frigate, sailed up the River Foyle to Derry – although they referred to it as Londonderry – one late November afternoon in 1965. This was my first visit to Ireland, although my Father had been born in County Cavan and all my brothers had spent their childhood there.

Several of the crew prepared for 'a run ashore' to explore. We had been regaled with stories of Derry's delights by more experienced seadogs. We spruced ourselves up for adventure and perhaps a dash of romance. First we had a thirst upon us and a drink was called for. The first pub we encountered was closed, as was the next, and the one after that.

Of course we were familiar with opening hours in England where the pubs closed between 2pm and 7pm on Sundays. This was Sunday, so assuming the rules were the same, we waited outside a decent looking establishment, as it was nearly 7 o'clock.

Along strolled a knowledgeable gentleman: "Yese will have a long wait there, muckers. There's no drink in this town on a Sunday. Yese will have to go into the Free State if you want one."

Of course none of us were aware of what he was talking about. My knowledge of Irish Geography/History/Culture was very limited in those days. I just knew it was my father's birthplace and that it was a place he always spoke of returning to. He had passed away five months previously, having never fulfilled his dream.

After a short discussion four of us decided to invest in a 'fast black' – a taxi that would take us into this strange place called the Free State. The hackney driver inquired if we wanted to go down to Muff or over to Bridgend?

Well, as the sniggering died down in the back of the taxi, four virile, sex-mad, young sailors unanimously elected to go down to Muff! We commenced our journey and shortly afterwards, the driver stopped the car and went into an official building carrying his logbook. On his return he started the car and drove on for about 50 yards. He cranked down the window, leaned his head out and spat copiously onto the ground. We had crossed the border! I had arrived in The Republic of Ireland, for the first time in the 21st year of my life.

"Here ye are lads – The Squealin' Pig, now enjoy yerselves and remember to be careful," our chauffeur advised, as he extracted an exorbitant sum of money from each of us.

Several good drinks were enjoyed in that packed bar and the craic was mighty, as they say; then at about 9.45pm a bell rang and someone shouted "last orders." I couldn't believe it, I mean I was only getting started! The management was not backward in removing all the patrons come closing time – so we found ourselves on the street once more.

One of my companions was told that a dance was going on further down the street, so, still looking for drink, two of us decided to go dancing. We paid 10 shillings each to get in and entered the aptly named Borderland ballroom.

And once inside yet another shock! No drink! No bloody alcohol! Dancehalls in Ireland were not licensed, we were told. We could buy a mineral though – God preserve us from all harm. My shipmate hit the floor and danced with a very attractive girl, who apparently asked him why I wasn't dancing? He returned with a message that she would like to dance with me.

Now dancing was not my forte and still isn't; I have no sense of rhythm or balance. However, the hall was absolutely packed and this girl was a great mover; she had a terrific pair of legs, so I went over to her and we began to shuffle around the floor.

I remember everyone going mad over something called the Hucklebuck and I took particular delight in singing along with 'Up went Nelson in auld Dublin'. Coming off a Royal Navy ship, I thought this quite ironic.

During the course of our conversation, this beautiful and charming girl informed me that she had been to Mass and Communion that morning; I responded that "so have I." However I didn't tell her that my attendance was in the company of fellow sailors from the British Navy in Pennyburn church in Derry.

We celebrated our 50th Wedding Anniversary four months ago.

Brendan Moran hails from London but now lives in Donegal. He sailed the world with P&O and later joined the Royal Navy. He has two sons and a daughter and remains married to the "most wonderful girl" who ever came out of Borderland.

| 18 |

The Girl In The Red Coat

Michael Lynch

B ACK in 1961 I had reason to leave home to follow my work to a town about 30 miles away. It being the month of December there was no chance of playing a bit of football and as I didn't take a drink I never went to the pub, so it was the dances and carnivals that I enjoyed.

Carnivals were very popular in those days. They were usually held in marquees as most of the parish halls were too small to accommodate the large crowds attending. The carnivals ran from Easter to September and attracted huge crowds because this was the real showband era. The carnivals ran for at least three nights a week for about three weeks.

I stayed in digs in the town and I would walk home from work down the street every evening. So I got to meet the same people on a regular basis and bid them good evening. There were two girls in particular I met a lot. They gave me a friendly smile and I suppose I gave one back! There was one girl in particular I took a fancy to but I hadn't the courage to talk to her.

Eventually one morning I met her cycling towards the town and I distinctly remembered the red coat she wore. At least I knew now the area she came from but I was none the wiser about where she lived.

I was working then on the Rural Electrification around the country and it took us to many different locations. One day we were sent to connect up a group of three houses. At that time the five man gang would do everything; design the line, dig and erect the poles, put up the conductor and leave it ready for the meter.

My job on that day was to run the service cables from the pole into the house. I went into the hallway in this particular house to erect the meter and saw several coats hanging on the wall which were in the way of my work. The man of the house said it was ok to move them. As I did so I could hardly believe my eyes for there it was... that red coat.

What luck! And there was no doubt in my mind it was her coat. Now I had to plan where I might meet her and obviously a dance would be the most likely place. No dances were allowed during Lent, but I knew the

Betty Devenney's story (see Page 197) relates to her dad playing with the Melody Aces (pictured below) when they were one of the main attractions in the country. As the poster suggests, they topped the bill wherever they went.

Monster Christmas and New Year

DANCES
IN RAINBOW BALLROOM
GLENFARNE

Three Teriffic Attractions ! !

MONDAY, DECEMBER 26th
THE HIT BAND OF 1955

THE FABULOUS MELODY ACES

Featuring Top Vocalists David Coyle and Gene Tighett, you must hear them. Admission 5/-
Outstanding door prize, yes, it's a beautiful 21-piece tea set. Bus leaving Enniskillen at 7.30, Roslea bar at 7.35, Florencecourt
Inn 7.40, Mullaghdun 7.50, Belcoo 8. 0, Blacklion 8. 5.   Don't miss the bus ! !

FRIDAY, DECEMBER 30th
THE BILLY CAMPBELL BAND SHOW, DERRY

With first-class Vocalists and Compere.   Comedy and Novelty Features introduced.   You'll want them back.
Admission 5/-

SUNDAY, JANUARY 8th, 1956
Andy Hennessy And His Showband, Kilbeggan

Vocalists, three in harmony, Fred Warren, Johnny Dullaghan and Noel Kirby.   A treat for young and old.   Bus from Blacklion at 8.45.   ADMISSION 5/-

Thanking you for your patronage during 1955, and wishing everybody a happy Christmas and New Year.

I remain your obedient entertainer.

JOHN McGIVERN
PROPRIETOR

Brendan Bowyer and The Royal Showband at the Television
Club, Harcourt Street, Dublin, 8 January, 1968. In 1962
The Royal Showband released the first ever single by an Irish
showband, 'Come Down the Mountain Katie Daly' with vocals
by Tom Dunphy. Bowyer would later become one of the first
Elvis Presley impersonators. *Photo by Michael O'Reilly*

The Clipper Carlton Showband rehearsing for Radio Éireann's *Maureen Potter Show* in O'Connell Hall, Dublin, 1 November, 1964. Back row: Billy Brady (guitar), Pat Lynch (vocals), Art O'Hagan (bass), Fergus O'Hagan (vocals), Hugo Quinn (trumpet), Neil McMahon (sax). Front row: Paddy Courtney (drums), Maureen Potter and Jimmy Moore (keyboard). The band, from Strabane, Co Tyrone, is widely credited with popularising the showband style in the late 1950s. *Photo by Michael O'Reilly*

Right: The Clipper Carlton Band join Melody Aces and the Royal Showband in the lineup of entertainment at the Beechmount Ballroom in Navan, Co Meath.

Beechmount BALLROOM Navan

Ireland's Most Popular Dancing Rendezvous Ireland's Greatest Show Bands on the Stage. ALWAYS A GOOD BAND. ALWAYS A GOOD DANCE.

FRIDAY, 5th OCTOBER—

MELODY ACES

Dancing 9—2 :: ADMISSION ... 6/-

SUNDAY, 7th OCTOBER—

CLIPPER CARLTON

Dancing 9—2 :: ADMISSION ... 6/-

FRIDAY, 12th OCTOBER——
9—2 :: 7/6

ROYAL SHOWBAND

The Nevada Showband poses for a publicity still, Dublin, 14 December, 1967. Clockwise from front left: Will (Billy) Walsh (trumpet), Bunty Hayden (sax), Danny Ellis (trombone), Roly Daniels (vocals), Kelley (vocals), Liam Hurley (guitar), Jim O'Connor (bass) and Pete Hayden (drums).

Photo by Michael O'Reilly

Showband icon Butch Moore (The Kings Showband; formerly of The Capitol Showband) with UK dance troupe Pan's People, recording one of six inserts for RTÉ Television's *Top of the Night* series, 13 September, 1968. *Photo by Michael O'Reilly*

The Granada Girls Showband (left to right): Mary Morris, Stephanie O'Connor, Kathleen Maxwell, Ann Coleman and Mildred Beirne. See Mildred Beirne's story, Page 133

The Highwaymen Showband from Birr in Co Offaly, left to right: Peter Richie, Brendan Mulhern, Don O'Sullivan, Ken McDowell and Mike Davis.
See Brendan Mulhern's story, Page 110

Right: The Entertainment Guide in the *Evening Herald* newspaper from 1964 is dominated by showbands.

annual carnival would start in a local parish on Easter Sunday night which was not far away. Instead of going to a dance back home, I headed the 30 miles to the carnival where I hoped she might be.

The place was packed. I scanned the horizon and down the marquee to my great delight I spotted her. My problem then was to see if I could get to her in the rush before anyone else asked her out on the floor. I made a bee-line for her but when I asked her to dance what do you think she said?

"Sorry, someone has asked me to keep this dance for them."

I was so disappointed but there was something about the way she said it I knew it was not a complete 'no'. I waited patiently for the next dance and lost no time in making my way across the floor to her. This time to my delight she said "yes." I was with my lady in red and was I a happy man as I danced her around the floor.

We talked about different things and about people we both knew. She knew my landlady where I stayed in town. I was about to ask her could I take her home or could I buy her a mineral, which was the first step in getting acquainted, when she informed me that my landlady's husband had died earlier that day. I couldn't believe it because I was talking to him on the Friday evening before I went home for the weekend. Unfortunately that put romance out of my head that night!

However I returned the following Sunday night to try my luck again. She was there and I lost no time in making my way over to buy her a mineral, which she accepted. I danced with her several times that night to music of the Melody Aces and the one and only Seamus Hutchinson, one of the very best singers from the showband years.

Near the end of the night I asked if I could taker her home and boy was I a happy man when she agreed. I told her I had an old car and we made our way hand-in-hand to the Morris Minor.

It felt great to be able to hold the girl I had pursued for so long. I'll never forget the showbands and the carnival that helped me meet her. That friendly girl I met on the street, the girl in the red coat...has been my wife for over 50 years.

Michael Lynch is a native of Co Cavan and is a retired ESB employee. Married with eight grown-up children, he enjoys writing short stories and reading and writing poetry.

Making An Empty Hall Look Full

Pat Healy

D ANCEHALLS were in my blood; my father, Michael, built one out of the remnants of an old cowhouse and ran all other sorts of entertainment in it for years. It might have been only four concrete walls and a galvanised roof but it was the social and cultural fabric of this area for decades.

The early fifties was a different type of dance world to the one that we got used to with the advent of the showbands in the late fifties. The original Healy's Hall was heated by a turf fire and was serviced by dry toilets with an overwhelming smell of Jeyes Fluid.

It was the era before cars were plentiful on the roads. People either walked or cycled. The only drama I remember from my early youth was the night three sisters were 'pulled' by the local Garda for having no lights on their bikes. They came in crying to my mother that they'd be fined.

We grew up around this business and I suppose it was inevitable that in turn, myself and other members of our family would run it at various stages in our life.

In 1957, my father built a new dance hall to cater for the changing times. He wasn't a builder and hadn't pillars in to support the heavy asbestos roof. In the big storm of that year the walls came tumbling down but luckily no one was hurt.

It was a setback but the neighbours were great. They all gave him a day in the great *meitheal* tradition and the second time around, he built it properly.

People were dance-mad in our part of the world. They thought nothing of going first to Pontoon for a dance and then heading to Enniscrone later on the same night. I know because I often did it myself.

The big challenge was that there were several venues only a few miles apart around our place. Down the road was the parish hall in

Aughoose and a bit further away was PJ Garvin's dance at Carratigue Hall. There were three or four other dances on the same night as ours, including Ballycastle and Derrynameel which were only 15 miles away. We had to be clever and resourceful to attract the people through our doors, given the level of competition that was out there.

We are located in Glenamoy between Ballina and Belmullet on the north coast road and many cars would pass on those dance nights still wondering if they would pull in to us or keep going to one of the other attractions.

I came up with ways of making our place look and sound full of life. I learned that if you covered the windows, people couldn't see in and that meant they didn't know if the hall was full or empty.

Sound too was important and I'd direct bands to begin playing early and to act as if the floor was full even if there was no one dancing. That made it sound to those outside like there was plenty of action.

My mother, Bridget, played her part by writing to the car drivers in the area earlier in the week inviting them to our place and offering free admission and refreshments. The prospect of food, drink and entertainment for nothing was a trump card in getting people delivered to our doors.

Those drivers were important because inevitably with a shortage of transport, each could ferry six or seven others in their cars with them to the venue.

Their passengers would have to fork out the admission price but my mother would give the drivers the VIP treatment. First, though, she would get them to re-park their cars out along the roadside so that it looked to others passing that they'd be missing something if they drove on.

I lost count of the number of times we duped strangers in this manner. I still chuckle at the memory of watching them pay in only to hear them curse: "Feck, there's no one in here at all."

At that stage, they had no choice but to stay. We worked on the premise that like a flock of sheep at a gap, once one went through, the rest followed.

My mother's food and drinks operation was an integral part of the business. For two shillings, patrons could have all the tea and bread they wanted. However for four shilling, they got the deluxe version – ham, bread and tea until they could eat no more. I do not think she made any profit on the food side of things but it helped to attract a crowd each night.

The Parish Priest could be a problem if he made announcements about parish hops from the pulpit that were in direct opposition to us. Once she asked him if he could change the date of a dance but he refused.

She was angry at his stance, claiming: "That's alright for the PP but he doesn't have a big family to rear like us."

I learned the trade from her and my father and took over after I bought them out. I was the Jack-of-all trades in the business – putting the admission money into a biscuit tin, paying the bands out of it and making sure there was a few bob left at the bottom for myself at the end of the night.

I was also the bouncer but thankfully fights were few and far between because the places then were teetotal. Occasionally I'd see fellas come in with naggins of whiskey in their pockets. At the end of every dance set, they'd head off to the toilet to take a swig out of their bottles. After a few visits, some of them would begin to get frisky on a few levels.

I remember one night, a few of them began squaring up to each other but Roly Daniels, who was playing there that evening, winked at me and told me not to get involved.

It was good advice. It made me understand that if they wanted to fight, it was better to get them outside and that is what I did any time a punch was thrown.

Invariably 10 minutes later the lads who were at loggerheads would come back into the hall. After the few slaps and bit of pulling and dragging, they'd dust themselves down and become the best of friends again.

The arrival of the big ballrooms led to the demise of the smaller venues but we fought on. In fact, we're still there. I changed the dances to a Saturday night and it worked because the big venues were all competing head on every Sunday.

My mother always had it in her head to build a pub but she felt my father might end up her best customer and waited until we were grown up. The result is the Anglers Rest which is now a landmark watering hole in this part of the country for over 45 years.

I was in the business from the time I was a kid but in 1983 sold it on to my brother, Kevin, who had come back from America. He then ran it for 18 years before selling it on to our sister Bernadette McAndrew, who has kept the Healy name over the door. The dance hall is still going, but not every week – it would be more like once a month. But the main thing, it is still going and very successfully at that.

Pat Healy is a native of Glenamoy, Ballina, Co. Mayo. Married with five children, he retired a few years ago. He is interested in all sports especially Gaelic football.

Magic Of A First Dance

Pauline Brew

IT was coming up to my 17th birthday and I couldn't wait to go to the local ballroom in Effin. It was 1965. The showband era was in full swing and for a few years I'd been green with envy watching my sisters getting all dolled up to go dancing every Saturday night.

How was I going to persuade my father to let me go? Over the following few days I begged and cajoled him and made a lot of rash promises to do extra work around the farm. My winning argument was that my sisters would look after me.

Now I faced another problem – what would I wear? I couldn't go in the pleated skirt and blouse that I wore to mass on Sunday. Who in their right minds would ask me to dance dressed like that? My sister came to my rescue. She was really good at sewing. We decided that there was just enough time to make a dress. We bought a piece of material and cut it out on the kitchen table. It was a beautiful shade of red. We stitched and sewed until the small hours of the morning.

The dress had a high neck and sleeves down to the wrist. It had a lace collar. No plunging necklines in those days. Lycra hadn't been invented. I wouldn't have been allowed out the door in anything above the knee anyway. It was gorgeous. My sister gave me the loan of a pair of shoes. We stuffed the toes to make them fit. For the first time in my life I began to see the advantage of having older sisters.

One of my sisters was very sophisticated. Her hair and her clothes were always perfect. Not for her a homemade dress. She spent a week's wages on a beautiful shimmering creation. She got her hair done in the hairdresser's in the latest style.

The night before the dance I washed my hair and slept with the rollers in. It was self-inflicted torture. In the morning when my hair was nice and curly I thought it was worth the effort. I could not sleep anyway because I was too excited.

On the night we set off and about a quarter of a mile from the hall, we hid our bikes and walked the last bit on foot. We paid our admission and handed in our coats to the cloakroom.

My sisters had arranged to meet two fellows and promptly deserted me. However, there was a great atmosphere. When Dickie Rock appeared the crowd went wild with a troupe of girls gathered at the front of the stage. I had never seen anything like it. My sisters were in great demand for dances. They were asked up every time.

I saw a really nice boy approach. He was smiling and gorgeous. I smiled back. He asked the girl behind me to dance. The next boy asked the girl beside me. One by one they were all asked up. Then I saw a big hunk of a farmer's son coming. I prayed silently that he wouldn't ask me but obviously God had bigger problems to solve that night.

To say that he had two left feet was putting it mildly. All I could think of was that my sister would kill me if her shoes were ruined. We plodded on. The set, which consisted of three songs, ended and I limped back into line.

For some reason – maybe because I relaxed – the night took off from there. The band played one song after another. I was asked up for nearly every dance. A boy took me upstairs to the mineral bar and bought me a bottle of red lemonade.

After the interval the music reached a new high. The boy asked me to go outside. I had noticed that couples had been doing this all night. I wondered why they would go out in the cold when they could have stayed inside in the warmth? Such innocence.

I could also remember the nuns advising us about "occasions of sin." I wondered was this such an occasion? Bad enough that I had put my body through so much for this dance; no way was I going to put my soul in jeopardy as well.

I declined but promised I would meet him the following week. I didn't.

The band played over time and it was one o'clock when The National Anthem sounded. Panic set in. We should have been home half an hour ago. We grabbed our coats and ran to our bikes. The flashlights had been stolen off them. Luckily we knew our way home even in the dark. We arrived at the road gate. Just in the passage way through two more fields and we pedalled faster. Suddenly there was a thud followed by a scream; my sister who was always in control went flying over her handlebars. She landed with a squelch in a heap of cow dung. She had hit the black polly heifer side on.

Our parents were up but weren't prepared for the vision of their ultra-sophisticated daughter standing in front of them covered in cow dung. Her expensive dress was also ruined. They began to laugh. Everything else was forgotten.

As I drifted off to sleep I clicked the recall button to relive the magic of that night. While afterwards I went to and enjoyed hundreds of dances, nothing ever quite measured up to that first dance in Effin.

Pauline Brew grew up near Charleville, Co Cork but now lives in Limerick. She is married with three grown-up children and enjoys writing as a hobby.

21

Going Back To The Candy Store

Joe King

T HEY still ask me to sing it. Nowadays it's generally at family gatherings, weddings, birthdays and the likes of that. Sometimes my wife, Mary groans and lifts her eyes to heaven when they call out and request the Candy Store, but I sing it nonetheless, and when I do it's as if the years drop from my shoulders and I'm back there singing with the Kingstown Showband. It's as if I'm 27 instead of 87.

We played mostly to audiences around Connemara and sometimes up into Mayo. There were five of us in the band, including my late brother, Frank. We all had daytime jobs and played music at night. I was in the building game and it was a nuisance removing builder's tools and materials from the van and replacing them with instruments, speakers, mikes and amplifiers whenever we were playing. Invariably something went missing during that rushed switchover. The roads of Connemara were often pot-holed and rutted. I recall one night returning from a dance in Mulranny, in Mayo when we got a puncture. We sifted amongst the gear in the back of the van but couldn't find a wheel-brace. Myself and my brother had no choice but to jack up the van and use tyre irons to remove the tyre and to patch the tube in-situ. That might not sound like much today, but try doing it on a winter's night with the sleet from the Atlantic coming at you in horizontal sheets.

Before the arrival of rural electrification it was difficult to amplify instruments. Sometimes we'd disconnect the battery from the van and use it as a power source. On more than one occasion it wouldn't have enough juice left after the dance was over to start the engine so we'd have to push until it spluttered into life. Later we bought a small petrol generator that allowed us to separately charge a car battery.

We always seemed to be rushing to get to venues. I recall an occasion when the battery was discharged so we thought we might throw the generator in the back, start it up and power the battery as we drove along. We were smokers back then and it took us a while to realise that the fumes in the van were not just coming from our cigarettes but from the generator which had caught fire. Times like that make you glad that there was no shortage of water in Connemara.

The arrival of electricity meant we could ditch the generator and the battery and plug directly into the mains in dance and parochial halls. We were in great demand in those years doing switch-on dances around Galway and Mayo. These occasions were where the ESB had brought poles and cables to rural communities and transformed country life with the throw of a switch. It was usual for the local parish priest and local dignitaries to be present for the switch-on celebration. I remember what a great occasion it was when we played for the switch-on dance in Clifden.

All the band members could play a range of instruments, doubling up whenever necessary. Frank started out on the button accordion but later switched to the tenor saxophone when musical tastes began to switch from céilí to Rock 'n Roll.

The Kingstown Showband stopped playing in the mid-60s. It was becoming harder to balance family life and day-jobs with part-time musical careers. But music is a strange thing. If it gets a grip on you it never wants to let you go. We'd occasionally get together for sessions and family events.

Frank passed away 13 years ago. During the last days of his life he appeared to have lost consciousness. We brought music recordings to his bedside and played them to him as he lay there dying. His hands were outside the bedspread. During the course of our vigil someone noticed that his fingers were moving – he was forming the music patterns for the saxophone in tempo with the tune that was playing in the background. Even as he departed this life he was holding on to the music that had lodged so firmly within his soul.

I am 87 and I know, no matter what Mary thinks, I will sing the Candy Store whenever I am asked to. That's what music does to you, it never lets you go.

Joe King is a native of Clifden, Connemara. He is a singer and musician, who enjoys his retirement in the company of family and friends

22

You Can't Trust A Man On A Honda 50

Gerry Tuohy

S OME events you looked forward to, others you lived for, but the last night of the GAA festival, well, that was at another level altogether.

The week of the festival had a buzz about it, the carnival, the bonnie-baby competitions, the Carnival Queen, the slot machines, the swing chairs, all great stuff, but roll on Sunday. The big marquee rose like a cathedral out of the bog-meadow field; a feat of architectural engineering to equal the pyramids built on a field with a 30 degree slope.

Unknown and popular bands coming each weeknight to entertain the festival revellers. On each occasion the crowds getting bigger, building to the weekend and Sunday night and Joe Dolan.

That night was about best trousers and shirt, Brut and hair oil, and down to Murphy's on the main road to oil the pipes. Murphy's widely known for sweet Guinness, and as the evening rolls on the pints getting sweeter. Excitement hangs in the air as the local boys land in on top of you, bawling and shouting and bragging about what the coming night might hold. Everyone knowing how it would begin. Mulligan's bus leaving from the handball alley at eight sharp, but as plans go, nobody with a clue about getting home.

Johnny 'Dry' is my banker, not only is he tee-total, he has a Honda 50! Rounds of pints are dripped up onto the bar, swallowed fast, and my head is dizzy trying to cope with what remains to be consumed before the 10 to eight shout for the bus.

All aboard Mulligan's marquee express, with a smell of perfume and beer as I try to hold my porter down and chat up the O'Driscoll girl. Not much joy there. She barely acknowledges my presence.

At the next village a dozen more climb on. Village after village, more bodies on board until we finally reached the marquee field. Bladder bursting. Off the bus into the throngs of people buzzing around, and the muffled sound of some showband coming from inside the marquee.

Empty the bladder into the briars and meet up with the gang at the corner of the field. I buy another bottle. The lads are having fun slagging the corner-back for the kick-pass across his own goal that lost the match the previous weekend. After that subject is exhausted and we're topped up with Dutch courage, we cross to the marquee where it's game on.

Along one entire length of the marquee is what we came for...the glamour! Beautiful women, young and old in their finest. Along the other wall is a gathering of men in their Sunday best looking for the most part like a bunch of calves awaiting their first sniff of fresh grass after months in the shed.

Up on stage, the support band finishing their set, the roadies moving the sound system around and then..."Oh me, Oh my..." Joe boomed from the stage and men charge across the floor. "D'ya wanna dance?" could be heard as they scramble to partner up. The Bourke lads are spinning around the poles in the centre of the tent. Tommy Bourke has his legs outstretched like a Russian gymnast. Temperatures rise as hit song after hit floods the marquee. The trumpets blast out 'Different Eyes, Different Sighs'. The condensation's dripping down off the roof and we're sweating with not a care in the world.

Newly matched couples sneak out the door as jealous 'work in progress' couples look on, knowing exactly what's going to happen in the electric darkness.

A small interval for the band as Micko hits the stage telling us that proceeds from the week's festival had raised enough to build a toilet for the GAA club.

Then it's back to the music and the calves stampede again. Different groupings, new alliances forming as the night rolls on getting ever closer to the National Anthem.

Joe ratchets the excitement further with 'Sister Mary.'

I've nearly danced myself sober, another try with the O'Driscoll girl and, I can't believe it, success. She'd love a mineral. The music's ending and all thoughts turn to the dreams of what might be. Johnny 'Dry' makes an appearance and offers both myself and the "particularly beautiful" Miss O'Driscoll a lift home. How's he proposing to manage this on his bike?

"Easy," he says. He'll drop her first. She can wait for me near their front gate while he comes back for me. Johnny's my mate and as he says, isn't it only 10 minutes each way.

I watch them both disappear down the road. See the lights of the Honda 50 blink goodbye and notice how tightly she is holding onto Johnny's waist. An hour later and I am climbing up the steps of Mulligan's marquee express – all on my lonesome.

I'm feeling hard done by until the bus begin singing "Make me an Island" as if we are all dressed in white and as good at warbling as the Mullingar man. Soon it becomes infectious as everyone of us start belting it out as if our lives depended on it. "Beat that," as the man says!

Gerry Tuohy lives in Kilmacanogue, Co Wicklow and has a great interest in the creative arts. He enjoys writing, photography, garden design and art. In his spare time he has been known to attend the odd Gaelic match when not out on the golf course.

| 23 |

Playing All Sides
With Rebel Kingdom

Michael O'Carroll

MY father was the leader and manager of a part-time showband called 'Rebel Kingdom' in Cork City from 1958 to the mid-sixties.

The name came from the fact that he was from Tralee and because he now lived in Cork City, he called the band Rebel Kingdom.

The individuals in the band all had day jobs and earned a few extra quid playing music. Normally they played only one night a week – on Sunday. Practice night was usually held on a Wednesday in our kitchen. My father had the job of getting the gigs, organising the transport to and from the venue which generally was a Volkswagen mini bus. Two of the halls they played were The Rainbow Ballroom in Ballincollig and The Parish Hall in Douglas. On a few occasions they played in a hall in West Cork where they had to use a supersize battery to power the amplification, as there wasn't electricity in the hall.

My father bought his sheet music in Crowleys Music and Instrument shop on Merchant's Quay. He would then enter the notes in tonic solfa (D, R, M etc) for those that could not read such notation. On the odd occasion when a new song was in the charts and the band were not sure how the tune went, a microphone would be brought in to my bedroom to get me to sing the song. I had a good ear for music and could pick up the air of a song from the radio very quickly.

Part-time musicians would come and go from bands. My father and I spent many Sunday mornings driving around Cork trying to get a replacement guitar player or drummer for the night when the normal musicians were sick or got called into work. My mother told me that Brendan O'Brien sang a few times with the band before he joined the The Dixies with Joe McCarthy.

Michael O'Carroll is from Co Kerry but moved to live in Cork for a period before returning to his native Tralee. He now lives in Celbridge, Co Kildare with his wife and three grown-up children.

24

Blooming At The Rose Of Tralee

Brigid Daly

DURING the years 1975 to 1979, I was part of a group of fun-loving Kilkenny nurses who travelled to the Rose of Tralee festival and Lisdoonvarna for an annual camping holiday. It was the highlight of our summer social scene and the crack and fun we had at both places was unbeatable. We were all in our twenties, foot loose and fancy free and secretly hoping to meet Mr Right on our travels.

On the final night of the Rose in 1978, the group decided to go to the Brandon Ballroom to see Brendan Bowyer and the Big 8 band. Dressed in denim jeans and a cheesecloth blouse, I danced my feet off all night to "the Hucklebuck".

I took a break near the end but with no seat available I sat down on the lap of one of our male camping friends from Sligo. As we sat together laughing and having fun with my friends, a tall, dark, handsome lad walked through the crowd and asked me to dance. It was the last dance and as the gang I was with joked "your last chance." We danced around the ballroom to the magical songs before the music stopped and we all stood in awe as the newly crowned international Rose of Tralee, Liz Shovlin from Philadelphia, was presented to the excited crowd. I can still remember her beauty but also the fun and carefree feeling I felt that night.

When the dance ended I returned to my friends followed by my mystery-dancing partner, then one of the lads lifted me up and said "take her," "take her" as she is coming back to Tralee for years and never got a man.

While they were all laughing, he asked me for my name and number. I reached down for an empty cigarette box and scribbled down my details. We went our separate ways and I passed no further notice.

However, a few days later I came home from work one day in Kilkenny to be greeted by my mother saying "some Cork farmer phoned here today saying he had met the Rose of Tralee."

Seemingly, my good-humoured mother chatted him up before inviting him up to Kilkenny. I couldn't believe she had done this with a fellow that I'd only met for one dance. Secretly though I was chuffed that he thought I was the Rose of Tralee. He phoned again later that evening from the public phone in Kanturk and we arranged to meet at four o'clock in the square of Castlecomer the following Sunday.

I drove to Castlecomer half-thinking he might stand me up; but to my surprise I immediately saw the blue Hillman hunter he told me he would be driving.

He was shy about going to my home for supper but I insisted. Arriving in our farmyard in Crutt, I can still see my parents, Willie and Josie, coming out of the henhouse with a basket of eggs. They swiftly moved across the yard and gave him the warmest Kilkenny welcome. That evening my entire family, including two aunts who were missionary nuns, sat around the Stanley cooker in our kitchen.

It was a baptism of fire for this poor Cork man, and if all this wasn't strange enough for him, by the end of supper my sister Margaret – who was getting married the following year – invited him to her wedding.

As the evening wore on I had enough of my family trying to sort out my love life, so I gave my sister an earful in our back kitchen, claiming that he wouldn't be around for her wedding.

Later on that night we went to see Foster and Allen, all dressed up in their leprechaun suits in the nearby Swan pub. We had a good night but as the distance between Cork and Kilkenny was unrealistic, we made no plans to meet again.

To my surprise each week the postman brought a letter addressed to me, in beautiful handwriting with lovely sentiments. Impressed by the attention I kept up my replies. On a cold snowy day before Christmas a parcel arrived and to my delight it was a beautiful card and gift set of perfume called 'Tramp.'

Girls of my era will remember that fragrance with affection. Well, that gesture swung it and I wrote and thanked him for the gift and invited him to Kilkenny for St Stephen's night in 1978.

We were married three years later and every wedding anniversary since I've never missed putting on my wedding dress.

I also love to look at the note I wrote with my details that first night back in the Brandon Ballroom. We joke and laugh about the way we met, the happy camping friends, my mother's good humour and the Tramp perfume that finally decided our fate.

Now 39 years later we have a wonderful extended family of seven. And having been brought together by the Rose of Tralee, Charles and I were so happy when our daughter Teresa was selected the Chicago Rose of Tralee this year.

Talk about writing a whole new chapter in our story of love and life but that's what that festival has done for us.

Brigid Lyng Daly lives on Allow Farm Kanturk, Co Cork, married to Charles, a local dairy farmer. They have a grown-up family of two sons and a daughter. Now retired, Brigid enjoys writing short life stories and is a singer with the Duhallow Choral Society.

25

The Hall That Once Was Lives Again

Tom Byrne

WHEN we were teenagers the focal point of social life in our corner of Carlow was the dances in Garryhill Hall. The hall had been in existence since the 'emergency' when the local unit of the FCA built it for their training sessions.

It was a long timber structure with low horizontal trusses supporting the roof. There was an extension built at the end which served as the mineral bar and was grandly named the 'tea rooms'.

The emergency, if it ever existed, was well and truly over when a group got together to run the hall as a local amenity. They had the usual events such as card games, meetings, the odd concert, the annual Goose Club, céilí dances and what were then called 'socials'.

This was about the time that the showbands were hitting the road and the 'socials' were falling out of favour as the young people wanted to be part of the new craze.

After long deliberations the committee decided to bring a 'promoter' on board to engage some of these showbands and make better use of the hall.

The promoter was duly selected and it turned out that he was a larger-than-life character. A Jack of all trades. He did a bit of trading by way of bringing butter and cases of whiskey from the north, he bought and sold pigs and bonhams to the local farmers, had a stall at the field-day or sports meeting and liked to get involved in anything where there was a few bob. As a result of these activities he was known the length and breadth of Ireland and this was no harm when it came to promoting dances.

He took to his task with gusto and turned out to be a natural for the job. He hired local bands such as the Roulettes, The Barrow Boys, the Tropical Showband, and the 'The Sailors' from Carlow. Business was booming with capacity crowds every weekend so he upped the stakes and went for the bigger national names. He brought bands from the surrounding counties such as the Davitt Bros from Wexford, Donie Cassidy with the Firehouse Showband from Westmeath and the Gallowglass Céilí Band who played a mixture of music to suit dances for the older couples.

He also brought some guest artists along including Joe Lynch who would later star as Dinny in Glenroe. Joe, who was a radio celebrity at the time, arrived in Garryhill in his Volkswagen Beetle, complete with his sheepskin coat. He was introduced by Dermot, the leader of the Roulettes, as they backed him singing favourites such as 'Courting in the Kitchen,' 'The whistling Gypsy,' and 'The Cottage by the Lee.'

Joe went down a treat especially with the women, who mobbed him in the 'tea rooms'. He then left to go to his Beetle, but when he started it up, and put the boot down he found he was going nowhere. Upon inspection he found that the go-boys had put it up on timber blocks. The same lads were watching from behind the hedge taking delight in Joe swearing about the pups that were in this God-forsaken place. The promoter was alerted and came to his rescue and sent Joe on his way with a fat fee.

When these bigger attractions were in town the hall would be full to capacity and beyond, resulting in sweltering heat with the crowd bumping into each other. This meant that there was liberal use made of the outdoors with blokes taking up position on the grassy bank, the bonnets of cars and the low granite wall that ran along the adjoining road, to partake of any extracurricular activities that might arise.

The promoter was by now a celebrity in his own right and lapped up the fame. If he had a drink on board he was known to take to the stage and give a rousing rendition of Phil the Fluter's Ball. Once when Bridie Gallagher was in town he had no inhibitions about doing a duet with her, singing 'The Boys from the County Armagh' and 'The Homes of Donegal'.

Sometimes he just couldn't be stopped until the band upped the tempo till he ran out of breath shouting: 'Jaysus, you'll be the death of me'.

The promoters side-kick was Sonny, who did all sorts of jobs from hauling in the cases of minerals, taking the money at the door, acting as chucker out if there was a disturbance or if the lights went out he was on hand to cobble something together to get the show on the road again.

The 'promoter' didn't have it all his own way however when it came to performances. There were a few gents who saw dancing as a side-show as they took the opportunity to perform their own speciality. One guy's act consisted of hanging out of the timber trusses and then propelling himself Tarzan-like from one end of the hall to the other while the crowd cheered and the band looked on in amazement.

As one end of the hall structure was higher than the rest, he would do the 'Wild Cat' down that end. However, one night in his enthusiasm he attempted it at the lower part and his long legs got stuck in the ceiling and he fell on to the floor.

Another bloke called Phonsie arrived the worst for wear with his shirt-tail hanging out. He would survey the ladies along one wall before asking one of the better dancers up. Then he would give an exhibition of 'The Twist,' the Hucklebuck or the 'Limbo Rock.'

Phonsie had amazing agility and could bend over backwards and walk under an imaginary line to the urgings of the onlookers. His legs seemed to be made of rubber as they wriggled like a dancing doll; he became known as 'Haley' – a name that stuck with him for years after.

There was another guy called Butty whose stunt was to juggle a couple of tumblers and then take a bite out of each before spitting the bits of glass out into his hand.

He would then drink orange squash from a long tube that he took from his trouser leg, pretending to wash down the glass chewings. The girls ended up screaming and running for cover in the mineral bar as they couldn't bear the sight or thought of him injuring his insides with the glass pieces.

With no drink served at the dances, patrons had their fair share on board before arriving. This in turn led to bouts of fisticuffs. There were a few blokes who loved nothing better than to be in the thick of a good fight as they saw it as a badge of honour or a way of impressing the girls.

The old hall is gone now but it still lives on in the hearts and minds of those of my generation who cut their social skills there, those who met their partners and made friends on those balmy nights in the sixties and seventies.

However the tradition of dancing in our part of the country hasn't died out with a revival of dances in another hall a short distance away where the young and the not so young can still be found dancing the night away, and who knows but there might yet be a few matches made there too.

That Hall that once was lives again.

Tom Byrne is from Garryhill, Co Carlow. Married with four grown-up children, his hobbies include local history and creative writing.

The Charge Of
The Night Brigade

Tom Rowley

BIG Tom wrapped hands as big as shovels around the microphone. I could see him out of the corner of my eye ambling forward on the stage, the cream suit edged in maroon braiding, the big mop of hair and the creviced, craggy features.

Behind him the Mainliners, dressed in similar outfits, were strumming guitars gently as a one-two-three beat began to grow and pulse. It was going to be a slow set and this was my chance to make a move. If I got there and she said 'yes' we might get close. I might even be able to pluck up the courage to ask her if she'd like a mineral.

If it had been a rugby match it would have been called a rolling-maul, on the Gaelic football and hurling front commentator Michael O'Hehir would have said a 'right shemozzle' was taking place. Men and boys, ten deep, were pushing, barging, elbowing their way forward in a frenzied stampede towards the girls lined up behind a waist-high barrier. I was stuck in the middle of it, nervous, shy, a bit scared, caught between whether to grind forward or try to scramble back out. The courage from earlier pints was seeping away, the sweat was slowly darkening the collar of my new purple shirt.

Then another heave as lads at the back dug in bull-headed and sent us all headlong towards the women. I was catapulted towards the front and propelled up against the barrier. I was facing the ladies and the crush from behind left no gap to escape.

And there she was. Fidelma. She wore white patent knee-high boots and a purple mini-dress that clung tightly. She had hazel-brown eyes, gentle rounded features and lips, kissed with a veneer of red lipstick. And boy did I fancy her big time?

She worked in a newsagents shop in Castlebar and any chance I got I was in there leafing through magazines and hoping she would notice me.

She was a year or two older than me, something that only added to her charm in my naïve quest.

Most of us in the charge of the night brigade were lads from surrounding villages who had headed into town for the night, walking, cycling or in my case crammed seven tight into a neighbour's Ford Anglia. Our dress for the most part was conservative – suit, shirt and tie and sensible shoes. Here and there the flap and swish of flared pants on those who wanted to be seen to be 'with it' on the fashion front.

There was an awkwardness about some of us. I was 17, a boy throwing the shapes of a man, and underneath the nerves and doubts swirled and churned. We were the young ones taking the first faltering steps. Mingling with us were, what we looked upon as, the ould fellas, bachelors creased by years cutting turf on windswept bogs, saving the hay in sun bleached meadows and scything through fields of oats and barley.

The pints beforehand gave them courage, the naggin of whiskey in the jacket pocket there to top it up.

The townies were another breed altogether, smirking at our efforts, and falling over themselves to portray sophistication. Leaning nonchalantly against walls, dragging on Carroll's Number Ones, casually flicking ash from velvet lapels, admiring the tightness of their Drain Pipe trousers and the reflected gleam off their Winkle Picker shoes. At least that was how we saw them. And always at some stage during the night a few of our lads would crunch fists and vow to sort out one or other of that namby-pamby set.

The Royal Ballroom in Castlebar, was better known simply as The TF as it was part of The Travellers Friends Hotel. A hot August night in 1971 and well over 2,000 souls of all ages, shapes and sizes had wedged their way in. On the dance floor a few married couples slid around gracefully, smooched close and here and there girls danced with each other, trying to avoid the impending stampede from the men's side.

It took a while before I finally plucked up the courage to ask Fidelma to dance. As I was half-way through asking her onto the floor, a tall sturdy fella in a white suit, Brylcreemed hair, frizzled sideburns and lathered in 'Old Spice' elbowed me aside and went straight for her.

She glanced at me and then shifted her gaze to look straight at him. Around her a cluster of girls giggled at the unfolding scene. I felt they were sniggering at my failed advances. I pushed my way back into the still heaving and straining mob behind so that I could hide my embarrassment within the crush of bodies.

All I wished for right then, Devil or not, was that I was in Pontoon. During that madcap time ballrooms were built in all sorts of odd, remote locations. Pontoon topped them all, a great barn of a building dressed up as a ballroom, with sequined lights, speckles of colours from red, green and blue bulbs bouncing and reflecting from the mirrored crystal balls revolving below the ceiling. The radio advertisements had the jingle – "The best in the West is Pontoon".

Pontoon was closer to my village of Parke than the TF in Castlebar and I felt more comfortable there. I knew a lot of the girls, many were neighbours, so there was not the same fear of outright sharp rejection when you asked for a dance. And the journey to and from it, walking, cycling or wedged in the Ford Anglia, had a haunting, almost mystical feel. It took you on narrow roads through bog and barrenness, the scents of bog heather and wild flowers drifting lazily on the breeze and in the distance, rising high and pocked with subdued colours, the dark rolling Laragan mountain.

And then, as if Pontoon ballroom wasn't mystical enough already, the Devil himself dropped in. I had been reared on whispered tales of the famous appearance of the Devil in the Ballroom of Romance in Tooreen, near Ballyhaunis, back in 1954 and of the fear and dread that followed. My mother's distilled verdict was: "Them priests will try any auld trickery to stop the young people going out and enjoying themselves."

The Tooreen and Pontoon stories mirrored each other. A tall, dark and handsome stranger arrives at the hall in a sleek black car. The girls swoon at his appearance, deciding he's far too good-looking to be from around the area. He invites the best-looking girl in the hall out to dance, whispers sweet compliments into her ear and is edging closer when she looks down and instead of shiny shoes sees two hairy cloven hooves. She, as they say, takes a strong weakness and when she recovers the dark stranger has vanished. The Tooreen apparition of the dark angel was in the unenlightened days of the early 1950s but Pontoon was in what we considered the modern era of the 1970s when we had coloured television, fridges, holidays to the sun and 'free love' was spreading 'like the testicles of an octopus,' as one county councillor succinctly put it.

Again, I sought an answer from my guru, the mother. "It's them priests again," she fumed. "It's all a load of codswallop."

The TF on that hot August night in '71 was hostile terrain, a place where I had to grow up mighty quickly. Big Tom had just launched into "Dim lights, thick smoke and loud, loud music," when I was spun back towards where Fidelma originally was. To my amazement, she was still standing there, the geezer in the white suit by now having moved down to the front row of ladies.

Our eyes met, lingered and I nervously half-poked out a hand again. This time she smiled, gave the gentlest of nods and slipped through the chattering nest of ladies around her, dropping a few comments to them along the way, to join me on the dance floor.

"I told them I was feeling sorry for ya," she whispered as she broke into a giggly smile. "But that's not really true. I've seen you in the shop. You like to play at being the shy lad. Sure I know your mother, she drops into the shop whenever she's in town. If she could see me now she would tear strips off me for robbing her darling little boy from the cradle. Sure we'll give it a go, do you know how to jive?"

She smelled of 'Tweed' perfume which gave off an odd aroma that reminded me of the fly-killer spray we used at home. She jived like a woman possessed, her curly hair swinging widely from side to side. I later found out from her friend Geraldine that curly mane was the result of earlier preparation with a medium hot iron and the help of brown paper in her mother's kitchen.

As Big Tom signalled the end of that set of dances, I made my move. "Would you like a mineral?" I asked, suddenly feeling grown-up.

"Ah no", she said softly. "Sure we've only had a bit of a dance. But maybe next time," she added with a wink.

Next time. That was all I'd wanted to hear. Something to cling to. Joe Dolan and the Drifters were lined up for the following Sunday night in the TF.

Tom Rowley, a native of Parke, near Castlebar, Co Mayo, is a freelance writer and public relations consultant. He was for many years a senior journalist with 'The Irish Independent' and later a Government media advisor. He lives in Blackrock, Co Louth.

Running Bear Meets Little White Dove

Collette Bonnar

'SALTHILL, that's where we should go for the week in August," suggested our friend Miriam.

"Why Salthill?" my sister Carmel, and I chorused.

"Seapoint Ballroom," Miriam declared. "Guaranteed to get danced off our feet – floor to ceiling lads in Seapoint," she said with confidence.

"It will make a big change from The Ballroom of No Hope," I commented, referring to a local dance hall.

It was early summer of 1973 and we were planning the holiday of a lifetime. It was a toss-up between Ballybunion or Salthill. Miriam had done her research and apparently, Salthill and The Seapoint Ballroom was the place to go for the movers and shakers.

We arrived there on the August bank holiday weekend and Seapoint lived up to its reputation. We were spoiled for choice as each set came around. A surge of fellows swept across the floor, all grappling to ask us out to dance. As Joe Mac from the Dixies threw his drumsticks in the air, we danced the night away to 'Little Arrows'. We met a gang of five young bank officials from Cork who were up for the long weekend. I fell madly in love with the driver of the Ford Cortina – a very handsome lad called Anthony. On the Sunday, I wanted the night to last forever as we danced to Dickie Rock, belting out 'Simple Simon Says'.

Friday morning wore round, it was time to pack our bags, hitch back to Donegal and reality. "There's definitely more men in the west than women," Miriam said dolefully as we stood at the side of the road outside Claregalway. A Ford Prefect had just swished by, ignoring our outstretched thumbs as the rain began to pelt down.

"A lift at last," Miriam squealed as she spied a lorry coming towards us. "The guy is slowing down." We piled into the lorry, four hours later we were back in Lifford.

After our holiday in Salthill, we decided to up our game in the glamour stakes and splashed out on new gear. I bought a new dress and six-inch platform shoes. At home that evening, I tried on my purchases. As I twirled and preened for my sisters, I thought I was Lifford's answer to Priscilla Presley. But alas, I was knocked off my perch the following Friday night at the Fiesta Ballroom in Letterkenny. The lead singer with the Indians, was singing 'Running Bear loves Little White Dove'. I thought lucky for Little White Dove as I stood like a wallflower – not even a single dance for the whole night. My sister and friends weren't having much luck either. We skulked off to the supper room to lick our wounds and find solace in egg and onion sandwiches, washed down with milky tea.

We stepped up our glamour strategy with due diligence. I bought a pair of white crimplene trousers, a white blouse and a purple suede waistcoat completed the look. With my hair well backcombed, I thought I looked a dead ringer for Priscilla as I headed off to the dance in the Butt Hall to hear Larry Cunningham and The Mighty Avons.

I smiled demurely as a dashing, fair-haired young man came in my direction, "Would you like to dance?" He asked in a deep-masculine voice. I was about to say, "Yes please," but the smile froze on my face as I realised it was the tall leggy-blonde girl who was standing next to me who had caught his eye.

Later, from my vantage point on the balcony, I noticed that the good-looking young man from earlier was still dancing with Blondie. Then her trousers caught my eye. The fabulous mega wide bell-bottoms. By now the pair were jiving to a quick set. Wow. I thought Blondie looked the bees' knees. Then I had an idea...

"Can I have a yard of the purple material?" I asked the sales assistant in Harley's Drapers shop in Strabane the following Saturday. I duly headed off then to the dressmaker to get her to do a little job on the white crimplene trousers.

Piling into the hackney on Thursday night, one of the girls gawped at my newly-modified trousers. They looked like a pair of loons, which resembled parachutes from the knees down. "What did you do to your good trousers?" she asked.

"I got them turned into bell-bottoms," I replied defensively, thinking of Blondie from the week before. The inserts to match the purple-suede waistcoat worked. I got a few dances and was actually asked to 'stay on.' My younger sister Catherine, also happened to meet a young man that night who'd asked her for another date.

Over the next few months, we met the two boys inside the dance hall. We had such a great fancy for them we were prepared to overlook their stinginess in not paying the admission fee. About two weeks before Christmas, I was dancing to the Royal Showband as they sang Mud's hit song, 'It'll be lonely this Christmas', little did I think just how lonely it would turn out to be. A few hours later, my boyfriend dumped me. Later that night when we returned home, Catherine told me tearfully that her boyfriend had finished with her as well. The pair of skinflints had made a classic move to get out of buying Christmas presents.

The summer came around once more. Brian Coll and the Plattermen were one of our favourite bands that played regularly in the Butt Hall. I remember walking down the street in Strabane one Saturday and spying a yellow dress in a shop window. A short time afterwards, I arrived home with the dress in tow and a bottle of Ambre Solaire – the perfect tan in just twelve hours.

That evening, I began the tanning process – the transformation of Little White Dove. I decided to ditch the instructions and lashed the white cream on with gusto. Later when the job was complete, I was bursting with excitement as I told my sisters: "I've gone for the big one – forget a Mediterranean tan, I'm going to have the Caribbean look in the morning."

Going to bed I was still milky-white. Oozing with confidence, I was picturing myself jiving in the new yellow dress, my deep-bronzed legs being the envy of the Butt Hall. The night had grown a tad chilly so I donned a pair of socks that came to mid-calf. I then hopped into bed. Burying my face in the pillow, I fell asleep and dreamt of meeting the man of my dreams at the dance the following night.

Next morning in the bedroom as I began to get ready for work, my sister Carmel howled with laughter, this brought my other two sisters rushing into the room.

"Quick, look in the mirror," they were shouting.

My heart sank at the reflection that stared back at me. I looked like a Zulu warrior. I hadn't bargained for the tribal look which was the result of my face being stuck in the pillow the previous night. The rest of my facial tan was decorating the pillow slip. But worse was to come. My sisters fell around the place laughing when I removed the socks.

"You look like you're wearing white wellingtons," Deirdre chuckled. "You'd better wear trousers to work."

"What about The Butt tonight?" I wailed, staring in shock at the socks which were a deep mahogany on the inside?

"Unless you go in a space suit, you'd be better staying at home," Carmel joked.

That evening as soon as I returned from work, I made straight for the bath but no amount of soaking would remove the botched tanning. I finally had to concede that The Butt was a no-go area that night.

As the week wore on, the tan wore off. To make up for my disappointment at having to wait another week to wear the yellow dress, I treated myself to a pair of white Roman sandals. Criss-crossed to the knee, they looked the biz with the new dress.

I'd gone to the hairdresser after work and had my long chestnut hair washed and blow-dried. As I set off with my pals to the dance I thought I looked simply irresistible. The fiasco with the fake tan was soon forgotten as a gorgeous fellow asked me to dance and 'stay on.' As it happened it was on that night in The Butt Hall, Little White Dove met Running Bear. Three years later we walked down the aisle.

Collette Bonnar is a retired bank official, married to Denis and living in Stranorlar, Co Donegal. She took up creative writing four years ago when she joined the Gateway Writers Group in Lifford.

| 28 |

Big In Cadamstown

Brendan Mulhern

IT'S strange how you remember things, I hadn't been to Cadamstown in years and the memories came at me like a freight train. It was the early 1960s in Birr and we formed a band that practised above the doctor's surgery. Doc Richie worked downstairs with his stethoscope and patients as covers of songs by Eddie Cochran, Billy Fury, Bobby Darin, and Elvis leaked through his ceiling.

We called ourselves 'The Highwaymen' after the American group responsible for the hit 'Michael Row The Boat Ashore'.

We were friends first and band mates second. Mike and Senan Davis were two members who lived just a few doors down from me on Newbridge Street.

The band really started with traditional music in the Davis' house. The Fleadh Cheoil was an annual event in Birr back then until Rock 'n' Roll arrived via Radio Luxembourg. That station and the BBC's Top 20 became our lifelines.

Soon afterwards the showbands arrived: the Miami, the Paragon 7 and my own particular favourite, the Donie Collins Showband.

We were in awe of the big names that travelled from Dublin and beyond to play in Offaly. They were a huge draw for our generation.

None of us could read music so everything we learned was by ear.

Mike Davis was brilliant on the button-accordion, but the thing is, Mike learned to play it upside down. Sometimes when we practised in his house we would rig-up speakers and hang them out the windows. People could hear Chris Barber songs drifting down the street towards Emmet Square. Mike's brother, Senan, played lead guitar and was lead on vocals. Money was tight but my parents bought a set of drums for me and the Doc's son, Peter, played rhythm guitar. Peter had contracted polio and to help him recover, the Doc asked if there was a place in the band for him. We were delighted.

One afternoon we were rehearsing upstairs in the surgery when one of the Doc's patients offered us our first gig – in Cadamstown Hall. None of us had a driving licence. We didn't even own a bicycle. But Dr Richie came to the rescue again to drive us. That first night we hired amplifiers from Bobbie Williams Electrical in Birr, piled them into a trailer and off we went.

The Doc became our roadie. Before we took to the stage that first night in Cadamstown we decided to include The Highwaymen's hit record on our playlist.

A decent crowd turned up and after we played 'Michael Row the Boat Ashore' people came to the stage asking if were we 'the real Highwaymen?' It was a nice moment but the real show-stopper was Mike Davis on the clarinet. His cover of Acker Bilks 'Stranger on the Shore' brought the house down.

After that night our reputation travelled from Clareen village to the townlands of Killyon, Banagher and Rathcabin. There were regular gigs in Birr at the Oxmanstown Mall, the County Arms and Egan's hotel as well as a Sunday night residency at Birr Golf Club.

The golf club had been in decline but a regular cheese-and-wine night accompanied by music from 'The Highwaymen' soon resurrected its popularity. However, it wasn't all plain sailing. There were differences of opinion and gigs got cancelled. I remember we were a no-show for one fundraiser in Clareen and the local vicar became so incensed he threatened to sue us. On reflection this signalled the beginning of the end for the Highwaymen.

Some of the band emigrated, another joined The Mighty Avons but only one ever hit the big time – our lead guitarist, Senan Davis. He was hugely talented and went on to play for 'The Conquerers'. They had a hit in the Irish charts.

At the height of our popularity we had gigs five nights in a row. We became so popular that another neighbour, Patsy Fitzgerald, approached us asking to be our manager. But by then there were lots of bands waiting to take our place.

I visit Birr now and again. The last time was when my sister was home from Canada. We were driving through some of the old townlands. In our heyday many of these places were haunts of The Highwaymen. No one in the car had the least idea of what the old music scene was like. I gripped the steering wheel, shook my head and tried to explain: 'We used to be very big in Cadamstown.'

Brendan Mulhern is a businessman from Birr, married to Lynne and in exile in Naas. He has two children, spends his free time in the garden, his evenings watching rugby on TG4 and his night's reading music autobiographies. He's at his happiest in record shops where he can lose himself wandering through old LPs.

Scramble In The Ladies Toilet

Seán Hallinan

I MUST confess straight away I never liked fellows who could jive or limbo rock like Chubby Checker and I detested those who could move their nether regions like Elvis. "Let's do the twist"... if in the future I meet the good Lord at the pearly gates the first question I will ask is: "Why did you create me-tone deaf and flat-footed. My mother could sing; my father's people weren't all crows and corncrakes, so why on earth did you not give me some small smidgen of musical comprehension?"

As an early teen in the mid-1960s I started out well enough. Not showbiz standard but I regularly rode our horse 'Rose' around our small farm singing with gusto.

In the following pubescent years I began to meditate a lot more on beautiful ladies and explore the lore of love. Thankfully elder siblings were fans of Radio Luxembourg and I was far more clued in to that, than to the nightly rosary religiously recited by my dear mother.

Then low and behold one Christmas in the mid-1960s an eccentric uncle's wife from England brought a record player and a bounty of vinyl 45s home – the Everly brothers, Buddy Holly, Jim Reeves, The Beach Boys, The Beatles and many more universal stars. "She loves you yeah, yeah, yeah". There were going to be great heady days ahead!

We started going to dances – four or five young bucks, braves from our village – in a blue Morris Minor that gained certain notoriety near and far. Five bob and an appearance of sobriety would get you past most door men. Mayo had a proliferation of dancehalls, the big ones – the TF in Castlebar, The Starlight and Pavilion in Westport, Claremorris and Ballinrobe Town halls and the more quaint country ones, some with paraffin oil and sugar on the dance floor – Aughagower, Frenchill, Islandeady, the Arcadia in Belcarra and many more. Foolishly in hindsight in the early days, happy-go-lucky and feckless youths that we were, we showed more interest in devilment than dancing.

One Friday night in Aughagower we dropped six eggs through the open exterior window of the crowded ladies toilet! The women dashed out into the hall whilst still adjusting their elastics! On another occasion one of us smuggled a leveret (a young hare) inside a jacket into the TF Ballroom and released him close to where the girls were bunched together. The first lady who spotted him thought it was a giant rat and she let out such a loud screech that you would swear she had seen the fellow from Tooreen with the tail and cloven hooves! The girls started to stampede towards the stage and breathless bouncers came running to check out the commotion. We nearly choked laughing and to this day I still have to smile when I muse on the confusion.

I wasn't making progress at the dancing stakes and I was often envious of my peers who excelled. I could get good marks at the slow waltzes (you bet). I was creative and innovative at the "shaking" but just barely passable at the Old Time Waltzes. Very regretfully the "Foxtrot" was a definite fail and "Jiving" and the "Siege of Ennis" were of a standard well beyond me. This of course diminished my chances with a lot of ladies as it's an established fact that all women – rightly love dancing. Without doubt many males considered dancing a necessary pre-mating ritual but wasn't it also 'art' in its highest form with the symmetry of two bodies moving in unison to a rhythm and beat.

I always had the right ideals and technique in my head but from the belt down there were problems and the feet could never deliver!

The pages in the ledger of our lives flip over quickly. In our late teens we sailed for Holyhead and we bid farewell to "Erin's green shores". The days of a slobbery kiss, a gable-end grope, old fashioned courting and innocent romance were coming to an end.

London had its share of Irish Ballrooms primarily packed with us male construction workers and multiple female nurses. The Galtymore in Cricklewood with its two halls – Céili and Country and Western, the Gresham, Camden Town, Kentish Town, Newcross (where once I got ejected for dancing with a chair) and later still the National on Kilburn Highroad were favoured weekend haunts.

There in that multi-cultural metropolis we stuck with what we knew.

"Butch – Walking the Streets in the Rain"; "Brendan – Do the Hucklebuck"; "Joe – White-washed Gable"; "Big Tom – Four Country Roads" and 'Spit on me' Dickie – with his Candy Store on The Corner" were all legends together with countless others who drew punters by the thousand to London Irish venues.

Some Irish folk, mainly middle-aged men, perhaps afflicted by a religious upbringing went to the pub to drown their insecurities in jugs of light and bitter. Theirs was surely a lonely existence – pub, digs and heavy construction work – a six or seven day ritual. The "light" of a laughing girl and the love and companionship of a female an experience sadly, they might never know.

I was luckier myself in that the seventies which were in effect my "roaring twenties". I learned a lot in the ballrooms, bedsits and bookie shops of North London. And how strange was it then that a decade later what transpired for me (best described by a quotation from novelist George Moore) – "A man travels the world over in search of what he needs and returns home to find it."

Seán Hallinan is a native of Co Mayo and is a keen GAA activist and follower. He is dedicating this story to the memory of his close friend, Gerry Mahon (1951-2016) – a true "Lord of the Dance".

| 30 |

Finding Cinderella
At The Maple Ballroom

Denis O'Higgins

IT was October 1971 when I received the official order from my job to
get myself to Monaghan within days. I barely knew that place before
the outbreak of the troubles in the North. That issue gave Monaghan a
rapid national prominence due to its pivotal location.

As I was attached to a small rural Garda Station in Waterford, the cross-
country journey up to Monaghan was a daunting undertaking. Having
packed all my worldly goods, including my dismantled bicycle into my red
mini-minor, I set out and it was late by the time I arrived in Monaghan
town on that stormy night.

My final destination was now only four miles away, but as I travelled
through the darkness, the journey felt much longer. I was aware that I was
near the border and worried I might inadvertently drive into Tyrone or
Armagh. Eventually I reached the last house on the row in Glaslough
village – my new accommodation. Despite the lateness of the night, the
friendly landlady was still up and waiting to welcome me.

The next morning I travelled the two-mile journey to the village of
Emyvale to commence duty. From 1970 that station had experienced a
major change from being a quiet one-person, part-time rural office to one
with a 24-hour operation. This meant there were 30 guards there, many
in their twenties.

Due to the troubles people further north came south to Monaghan for
socialising and even booked and celebrated their weddings in safety. The
local dance halls and hotels featured the top show bands and the
promoters were well financially rewarded with crowded venues.

When one of my colleagues suggested that I should take a spin to sample
the weekly dance in the village of Rockcorry one Thursday night, I
readily agreed. On arrival I headed toward the sound of music, but
when I put my hand in the pocket of my drainpipes to fetch my red ten-

bob note, I found nothing except a big hole which my precious cash had escaped through.

I retraced my steps back to my car and carried out a thorough search in my vain attempt to find enough change to make up the required ten shillings. However, when that failed, I spied my chequebook peering at me from under the seat.

I explained my predicament to the doorman and asked if he would accept a cheque. His answer was a puzzled glance and then he just ignored my request as if I was invisible.

When I didn't move away, two more officious-looking bouncers appeared. I related my "sad story" to them but was firmly told that it was against their policy to take a cheque. Entry was by cash only. I decided to hang around in case they changed their minds. It worked and after a private conversation between them, they relented. The deal was that if I produced my driver's licence they would accept my cheque and allow me in. Luckily I had that document with me and at last gained entry to the 'Maple Ballroom'.

This was an ordinary rectangular hall, mineral bar at one end and the band playing at the other. The ladies were bunched together on the right-hand side but looking at each other rather than across the floor. It gave the impression that they weren't interested in proceedings. The men, on the other hand, couldn't wait for the whistle to blow and made a mad run towards their spotted prey.

Sometimes, after good strategic planning when you did ride the tsunami to bring you face to face with your quarry, it was very humiliating to get a refusal. The walk back across that bouncy maple floor was a long and deflating journey.

However, I had my eye on my Cinderella and wasn't going to let the night pass without making my case.

I noticed that she got out for every dance with someone different and was still going late into the night. The trick now was to position myself properly so that when the dance stopped I wouldn't have to wade through the crowd. My plan worked and I was rewarded with a smiling "yes" from my chosen beauty. When "your next dance please" was called, I asked if she would waltz the floor with me again and she smiled another yes.

Luckily that was the last dance of the night, so despite all the waiting, I had made my strike exactly at the right time.

As it happened she lived on a road back towards Monaghan town. This presented an ideal opportunity to offer her a lift home, which happily she accepted.

I remember it being a very bright moonlight night but in my excitement when I started the car I couldn't find the appropriate switch to turn on the lights. Times were different then; and with very little traffic around, I started driving by the light of the harvest moon. Luckily within the first mile of the journey, I located the switch and activated my lights.

With all the fuss I forgot to ask her name, so after parting I wondered if I would ever manage to meet her again.

However, fate and determination decided that we did indeed meet – and we've been together every since.

Denis O'Higgins is a native of Knockcroghery, Co Roscommon but now lives in Co. Monaghan. Married with a daughter, he is a retired wildlife ranger and his hobbies include writing and travel.

31

A Window To The Stars

Elaine Bryan

MY memories of the showband era are probably different to many others. I was young when it was in full swing, but my sisters, Geraldine, Pauline and I grew up listening to the bands while sitting in our bedroom window and going to sleep with the sounds of the bands playing in our ears.

We lived in Callan, Co Kilkenny, as I do still, in the same house, situated right across from the parish hall. The late Fr. John Kennedy and his committee ran dances in the parish hall every weekend and held a festival for two weeks in August in a marquee adjoining the hall. Our late dad was, what you would now call, a bouncer but back then he was just one of the men 'looking after things' and our late Mam was 'on the door' in a ticket booth in the entrance hall taking the ticket money and stamping the 'pass outs'. These she stamped with ink and a pad onto the hands of the couples going outside for a breath of fresh air. Separately, of course, you'd have to be careful about who saw you going outside with someone in case word got back home.

We liked to sit in the window watching the comings and goings and style at the dances. Mam and Dad would occasionally come out the door and look up and see we that were fine or come over to check on us if we weren't in the window. My cousins Claire, Alycia and Ann were old enough to go to the dances and along with their friends, the Hogan sisters and the Kelly sisters from nearby Kilmoganny, they would all get ready in our house before the dance. Well, the clothes, shoes, curlers, make-up and hair spray that were all over our house was not for the faint-hearted and ... we loved every minute of it.

I remember Claire having a black sparkly flared jump suit. I looked at it for a full week before the dance. Hanging on the back of the bedroom door I thought it was the most beautiful thing I had ever seen. I couldn't wait to see her in it and yes when she was ready to go to the dance, she looked like Grace Kelly.

I recall one of my cousins telling us later that she was asked to 'stay on' with a fella one night but she was not allowed to leave the hall. Dad was at one door and his friend Jack Lyons was at the other and Mam was in the entrance hall. She was confined to a little booth with a window so my cousin crawled out on her hands and knees so Mam wouldn't see her. She didn't get caught... that time!

As we lived so near the hall, we were the first port of call if anything was needed; from a bread knife to a chopping board, to tea towels or any other necessity. I remember that among the glitz and glamour of visiting stars we had a visit from Tina of 'Cross your Heart' Eurovision fame. She came in to iron her dress for the stage performance that night, and no, we didn't offer to do it. Could you imagine burning it? Brendan Bowyer once got a phone call to our house and we had to run over to the hall to get him. I also remember that RTÉ's Aonghus McAnally, who I think was playing with Gina, Dale Hayes and the Champions, made his acting debut as the postman in Wanderly Wagon and had never got to see it on the small screen. So when Fr. Kennedy learned this he brought him over to our place. My sister Pauline sat and watched it with him on our television set.

The last year that they hosted the festival was 1979 and I was 14-years-old and that year Mam and Dad allowed Pauline and I to help serve the soup and sandwiches during the dance. Geraldine was allowed to go to dances by then.

It was the very last night and it was the great, late Joe Dolan and the Drifters who played. When we finished serving the refreshments, we were allowed into the marquee and I can remember everyone with hands in the air waving from side to side to 'Goodbye Venice'.

What a wonderful memory. It's my favourite Joe Dolan song ever since.

Elaine Bryan is a native of Callan, Co Kilkenny and has been Postmistress there for 25 years. Married with three grown-up children, she is a member of Callan Variety Club.

32

A Hair-Raising Tale From 'The Arc'

Rose Hegarty

IF only we had iPhones back in the sixties, I could relate the most hair-raising story ever told in Irish showband history. The incident took place in what was affectionately known by Corkonians as 'The Arc', the Arcadia Ballroom which was located in the city right beside Kent Railway Station.

The dance hall was a massive building with a very high roof and a separate, lower ceiling placed around the stage area for dramatic effect. This allowed the punters to look up and see the showband stars in a proper setting and it probably was better too for the sound from the microphones.

Virtually every week, we made our way to this mecca to see some of the top names in the music business at the time. For me there was no one bigger than Dickie Rock and when my friends and I heard he was playing, we looked forward to it all week.

I lived in the south side of the city – Ballyphehane – and most of my friends also lived down around the lough area.

There were no cars or lifts for us when we wanted to go into the city. We were only too happy to walk all the way.

It was part of the night out really that a big gang of us would start off on the south side and walk as far as O'Connor's Bar in Turkey Street, arriving at around eight o'clock.

We'd have maybe three or four glasses of lager and lime before heading down through Oliver Plunkett Street. I know this sounds a bit back to front but we'd often go into a little chipper there and have a bag of chips for 6d before the dance.

Then we'd walk down to the Arcadia and queue for admission. Invariably the place was packed. On one side you had the boys with their black thin suits and long hair with quiffs. On the other side the girls congregated in all their finery waiting for the main band to strike up. There was no drink sold on the premises but upstairs you could get tea, coffee or minerals and cakes and biscuits. These always tasted better if you met someone on the floor and they invited you up for such treats which were on offer.

Many groups, including the Miami, had dramatic ways of beginning their performances. Mostly, all except the lead singer, would come on, get their instruments set up and begin playing. Then as the dancers made their way out onto the floor, the star attraction would make his entrance and begin singing to huge roars and applause from the swaying multitudes below.

At the time, Dickie's song 'Georgie Porgie' was tremendously popular and as the band struck up the intro, all our eyes were trained on the side waiting for Dickie to come out.

The girls, in particular, loved Dickie and we were 10 deep at the front waiting for him. On queue, he burst on to the stage and jumped into the air.

However, whether the ceiling over the stage was lower than he was used to or whether his run and jump took him higher than normal, I don't know but something caught the hairpiece he was wearing – it might have been a hook – and he came down with less hair than when he jumped up in front of us.

I'd been to hear him sing a few years earlier and noticed that he was lightish on top. Now it wasn't that he was bald but he obviously was aware of the situation too and besides, the blond wig was more in keeping with his image as a pop star.

On the night his wig got caught, Dickie fled to the wings and one of the group retrieved the hairpiece and ran after him with it. The band played on and then some minutes later, Dickie returned to the stage, hair perfectly in place again, and was given an even bigger reception second time around.

Instead of pretending that the 'hair-raising' incident hadn't happened, he took the mic and smiled down at us saying: "I nearly lost everything there, didn't I?"

He brought the house down with that quip but then that was Dickie – everyone loved him and in my case, he is still tops. I was 65 this August gone by and arranged for my family to attend a Dickie concert for my birthday in Kerry, all wearing 'I love Dickie' teeshirts. Even my grandaughter Lily Rose got in on the act by learning the words of 'There's Always Me'... so we've another generation of Dickie fans growing up in our family.

Rose Hegarty is a native of Cork and is married with two children and three grandchildren. A massive Dickie Rock fan (see photo pages), she is a dressmaker and loves gardening.

Snowballs And
Handbags

Marian Devenish

AH, The Galtymore... will we give the 'Galty' a miss tonight? Not on your life! Fond memories of many a Saturday night – no, not many a Saturday night, every Saturday night spent there in the 70s and 80s.

The dance hall of hopes and dreams... and maybe a future husband? But not before we spent the evening at Biddy Mulligan's on the Kilburn High Road. We listened to great tunes and songs there and with rousing music in our ears, we'd head off down the road.

Imagine Cricklewood Broadway back then, alive with the leaking sounds coming out onto the night air from the featured show band and the green neon lights spelling out the word Galtymore. I recall how the upper window of the Galty ran the entire length of the frontage. You could see the trousered or stockinged legs of those in the upstairs bar looking over the balcony to the dance floor below. The long queues to get in, the serious looking bouncers eyeing up those who might have a little too much drink on them. Up the red-carpeted stairs to the cloakroom and finding a safe place to keep your cloakroom ticket – in your shoe, pocket or bag.

Next, into the carpeted ladies toilet area, heavy with the scent of Charlie and Mary Quant Havoc, (a Galty favourite), to re-apply a fresh layer of rouge and lipstick and be reminded of the acceptance of the 'three set dance rule or you're out' notice above the gilded mirrors.

Firstly a drink, ours was usually a Snowball or Cinzano and lemonade, and next a look over the balcony to see who you might put your eye on.

The next decision was which dance floor of the two in the Galty to visit first. Rightly or wrongly our late-teen selves regarded where the showbands played as the modern part. There we could throw a few shapes, dancing freestyle around our handbags, piled up like a campfire. The alternative was the other dance floor, known by some as the 'back field', where the céilí bands played traditional tunes for waltzing and set dancing. Here the many memories of home were palpable and often painful.

Following the announcement of "take your partners for the next dance please" the men surged forward like greyhounds out of their traps. The women were neatly placed on red-velvet, spindle-backed chairs waiting to be asked up. This sometimes amounted to a jerk of the head, a patois all of its own. Relief sometimes followed humiliation if you were left a wallflower while others waltzed by. But if you did get an offer you had to honour the three-dance rule.

One dance was an energetic jive, being twisted, twirled, spun, flung backwards, forwards around the floor like a lasso or a floor cloth and then being catapulted along the dance floor. In many instances you could tell that drink had definitely been taken.

The Galtymore Ballroom was a part of rural Ireland in North West London. I had experienced the complex ritual and choreography of similar dances as a young student many years previously when staying with relatives in County Mayo.

We'd hit the Starlight Ballroom at Carrowbeg on the Castlebar Road. There, we provided a grand buffet of women for the men to pick and mix... It was the same in Aughagower village hall.

In the Galty, the evening always ended up dancing and singing along with the showband music. I thought I was the belle of the ball as I took to the floor in my C&A blue shift-dress with floral inserts dancing to the strains of Bachman Turner Overdrives' – 'You ain't seen nothing yet.'

The showbands packed out the dance floor, the Indians especially. Great to see them still have the same energy when they came to the Leeds Irish Centre a few years back. Many a jive was done to Margo and Philomena Begley. More jiving to Big Tom and a date arranged to meet a young man at Golders Green the following week with a view to going to the Galty. He stood me up! But I headed for the Galty anyway.

And then 33 years later, making the monthly trip from Leeds to London to visit my elderly mother (who used to wait up for me in the early hours to hear about my night on the tiles). I overheard a woman tell that her sister had met her husband at the Galty 35 years ago and re-visited it some years back before it closed for good.

It really was an institution, a rite of passage. Maybe it's being resurrected in heaven with its balcony for us to look over and eye up the talent coming in and who knows, they might even still serve Snowballs?

Marian Devenish was born in London of West of Ireland parents in 1956. A teacher by profession, she is married with two grown-up sons and loves singing, dancing "and day-dreaming".

Old Ireland Meets
The New In The Bronx

Peter Nolan

THE year was 1979 and I was enduring a sweltering summer's night in the Bronx as the Fabulous Hi Spots Showband were murdering the Bee Gees from a stage set up on the pitch at Gaelic Park, the epicentre of Irish-American life in New York City.

Normally, the jiving, waltzing and Ennis siege-ing would have taken place indoors at the grandly monikered Gaelic Park 'Ballroom' but this was a special night. A fundraiser/send off for the New York Gaelic minor football team was being held, as the advertising poster had it "under the Stars."

Just 18-years-old and one of the honoured guests, I came in from Long Island for the big night. My cousin from Ireland, a year or two older, was my plus one. He was spending the summer commuting into the city from his aunties – my mother's – house while working in construction in Manhattan and kicking football in the Bronx.

We took the RailRoad to the Penn Station, hopped the A train to 168th, switching to the 1. From there to 238th Street, one stop from the end of the line.

Arriving at the Park we made our way to the bar, greeting my teammates, club and county, all the while. One New York player, from a rival club, a smallish guy already sporting a bit of a gut at 18, mentioned that he'd given up the drink in preparation for the trip and our match with London and then, we hoped, Down in the Ulster Championship. I nodded at the bottle of Michelob in hand. "This?" he laughed. "Nah, I meant no shots."

We wound our way through the bar and out into the oppressive Bronx night, commandeering a table on the playing field, a 14-yard free from the goalpost nearest the Gaelic Park entrance. It was there we set about drinking as many free pitchers of Bud as we could swallow, slagging the band and the dancers all the while.

Joining us as the third member of our little crew was the 16-year-old brother of a teammate taking advantage of the laissez-faire attitude exhibited toward underage drinking by the Gaelic Park staff on this festive evening.

Dancehalls and showbands, like most totems of Irish culture, had made their way from the old country to the new world, somewhat changed by the journey, if no less cherished.

An older generation spoke of the Jaeger House and The Central, proper ballrooms from the sound of it, that ruled the roost back in the 1950s and early 60s. In the telling, young men and women dressed up for their night out. Dresses for the girls, suits for the boys.

The music was a mix of Irish and big band. Sinatra and jazz.

But tastes change, scenes change and now the action had shifted from the glamour of Manhattan to the more gritty aesthetic of the Boogie Down Bronx. Dancehalls and showbands were on the wane with rock, disco and punk making both seem out of step with the times. But there was life in the old girl yet. At bars like The Archway, stashed under the Jerome Avenue El, and at County Association dances that occasionally recalled the old opulence, showbands still played and the dance floors were packed with young and old, Irish and Irish-American side-by-side.

At Gaelic Park, there was live music every Sunday after the matches and if the bands weren't céilí bands, they were showbands. Groups like the Hi Spots were in a tough place trying to keep the older folks happy while appearing cool for us kids.

And so we sat drinking glass after glass of beer while a group of middle aged Irishmen in white three-piece suits, á la John Travolta in Saturday Night Fever, bounced between Spancil Hill and The Bee Gees, throwing some old time rock and roll into the mix too.

They were good at it too, despite the occasional misstep. But for us, the night was just getting started. This was the burning Bronx of the late 1970s. If gentrification existed, we hadn't heard of it and it surely had no notion of setting up shop here.

Heady stuff, I'd imagine for a small town lad from rural Ireland. It was a lot for me too. I'd moved to the safety and sterility of the Long Island suburbs with my family nine years earlier but the lure of the Bronx, not always obvious to others, remained strong.

And so we ventured into the Bronx night guided by my fellow New York Minors, a country Irish lad and his American suburban cousin trying to hang with the locals.

One of our "guides," the youngest player on the team, was known as '21', a nickname he picked up because no one figured he'd live past that ripe old age. At 16, he sported a set of full muttonchops that gave him something of a wolf-like appearance, an effect that was only amplified when he leapt up onto the bar and howled like Lon Chaney on the night of a full moon.

The same '21' would perform his party piece for the good people of Tuam, County Galway the very night we pulled into town not long after our 'Under the Stars.' It was not well received.

Inevitably, the New York City night gave way to another brutal summer's morning and so we made our way up to the Grand Concourse where a different cousin had a bed, a couch, or maybe a patch of carpet for us. The Bronx was like that.

Falling out of the taxi we tipped the cabbie extravagantly and went in search of sleep. After all, now that our dance night was over, there was a match which had to be played.

Peter Nolan is a native New Yorker with strong Irish links. He is married with two children and is a journalist and short story writer.

| 35 |

A Cycle Of Love

Declan P Gowran

EILEEN was the first woman to seduce me but being only 12 at the time, I never really knew it.

She was a stunner and a mover. Her hips swung when she walked, and her hair bobbed. She was fairly fit and lithesome then, blooming in her early twenties. She was tall with short straight ebony hair, framing her face. She had a vivid rosy complexion and a pair of fiery eyes that bulged with curious passion. When I crossed her she would dare me, standing with her hands on her hips, legs apart, leaning to one side and tapping a foot on the ground. When she scolded me she stood in the exact same way while wagging her finger at me. Luckily my big brother Jimmy and I didn't rile her too often. But sometimes we would tease her to get her to chase us around the garden of Carrigeen Cottage.

"I slept like a log last night," I yawned.

"So if you slept like a log," Jimmy groaned for we shared the same bed: "how come you were kicking me all night!"

He showed Eileen the back of his legs: "Just look at those bruises."

Eileen bent down to nurse him, rubbing his calves: "There, there Jimmy, sure ye're bound to survive."

"Uuuhh! That was nice." Jimmy cooed: "Would you mind doing that again!"

"Why, ye cheeky coot!"

Eileen let fly with the dishcloth as Jimmy dashed for the door. Then she was after him like a flapping swan, chasing him around the garden and Carroll's field. She was laughing, he was laughing and I was laughing too.

Eileen taught us the rudiments of Irish Dancing in Carroll's kitchen to the sound of Céilí music on Radio Éireann. First she would demonstrate the steps of a plain reel. I would watch her lustily for I so wanted to be her partner: "Right foot forward, toe to the floor, left heel backward, heel to the floor: now both angled back and ye're ready, a stor! Dee dah, dee dah, dee, dee, dee... Seven steps to the right with yer hands on yer hips, reverse to the left, toe to the floor, heel behind and ye're ready for more!"

She was a natural instructor and I was the besotted pupil. That year Eileen wore plaid dresses tartan or patterned. She loved to dance; but then country folk loved to dance whether impromptu in the kitchen or the barn or in the local Ballroom of Romance.

What changes a year can introduce. Next time we went on our holidays to Carrigeen Cottage, Eileen's fashion had changed utterly. Now she hummed popular songs, jived around the kitchen to the trembles of trumpet, trombones and saxophones, blaring on the radio. She wore a swing skirt, flouncy blouse, short socks and Plimsolls with matching make-up and a pony tail for the Saturday night dance.

Carlow was then the hip town with ballrooms in hotels like the Dolmen, Croftons and the Royal where all the nascent showbands like the Freshmen performed. Eileen would cycle to the N9 at Castledermot to pick up the special dance bus which brought her and her pals to Carlow and back again before cycling home fully flushed and exhausted from her bee-bop exertions.

All went fine until one night in the misty early hours, Jimmy and I were awakened by the insistent honking of a car horn. Peeping out the window, we saw a green Morris Minor parked at the gate of Carrigeen Cottage with the back of a bicycle sticking out of its rear. We feared the worst – that Eileen had come to grief somehow on the dark country roads. Then we heard her high-pitched laughter.

Eileen had suffered a double puncture cycling home on loose chippings that were used for resurfacing a particular stretch of road. She was pushing her bicycle the rest of the way and rounding the last bend near home when the Morris Minor approached on her side.

Whether Eileen was dazzled or alarmed she instinctively jumped into the ditch as the car arrived, braked suddenly and stopped. The driver alighted and introduced himself as Lar, and at the same time offering his profound apologies as he pulled Eileen out of the ditch somewhat dishevelled followed by her bicycle which he stowed astride his car boot, before bringing both home safely. Lar had red wavy hair, a chirpy smile and bright rabbits eyes.

Jimmy and I could just about discern their conversation from the cottage: "Well Eileen, ye could always come to the next dance with me in the car, if ye like. 'T'would be safer if nothing else. How about it. Is it a date?"

Cute Eileen considered his proposition for a moment: "Well now, Lar," she insisted: "I need that bicycle for getting about and doing my chores so if you might help me fix those punctures, I might very well consider your proposal!"

A year later Eileen again said 'I do', and she and Lar danced happily ever after.

Declan P. Gowran lives in Dublin and is married with four children. He has two grandsons and one granddaughter. He is retired from Dublin Bus as a driver and Tour Guide. He enjoys gardening, reading, and writing. He has been an avid dancer since he was a boy.

Bringing The House Down in Manchester

Mildred Beirne

IT was like going from Riverdance to Spice Girls but that's what we did when we became the first Irish all-girl showband back in the mid-1960s. One week we were The Old Cottage Céilí Band, the next we were filling halls all over the country under the 'Granada Girls Showband' name that our musical director had thought up for us.

His name was Leo Beirne and I first made contact with him when replying to an ad in the Western People. He was looking for a singer and I was cocky enough – at 17 – to think that I could fit the bill. I got the job and then about three weeks later I also became the band's drummer.

There were five of us in the group – Mary Morris, Stephanie O'Connor, Kathleen Maxwell, Ann Coleman and myself, Mildred Regan as I was then. We were all 19 or under.

Our all-girl format was obviously very novel but Leo insisted that every girl had to be a proper musician before allowing us into the band. We could all read music and play several instruments. I also played the sax. It is no idle boast to say that we could play as good as the best around that time.

We became the main attraction wherever we went with a relief band on before us. Now in truth, we weren't quite as big as Dickie Rock or Butch Moore but we weren't far off it. We were a country and western outfit and we did a lot of Hank Williams, who was very popular in that era.

We got to play the top venues all over Ireland. We travelled by minibus and then we extended our reach across the Irish Sea to England. We became very popular because we appeared in all the major Irish centres.

Showbands were so popular that it was not uncommon for us to come across other groups on the road returning from gigs in the middle of the night. We often pulled up and chatted for 10 or 15 minutes before driving on for home.

I'm sure there were plenty of relationships struck up too and myself and Leo also fed on the music of love and ended up getting married in 1966.

It posed a dilemma for the other girls in the band because we had our secrets which we didn't share with our manager. Now that I was engaged to him they made me swear that I wouldn't tell Leo they smoked behind his back. Obviously that secret was safe with me.

Leo was from Galway and we settled down in Loughglynn in Roscommon where we raised our two children, daughter Maria, and son Leo junior, who now lives in Wales but I'm happy to report has turned into a good drummer. Maria is a brilliant dancer and followed in my footsteps as she teaches both music and dancing.

My husband sadly died 30 years ago after a long illness and I had no choice really but to take over his music teaching role.

It was really a matter of survival. Leo had taught music in Loughglynn School and the first day I went down I sat outside lacking the courage to enter. The principal, Mrs Bruen, came out and grabbed me by the arm and told me to start teaching. I did and to this day I've never looked back.

Since then I've been very busy and fulfilled, bringing music to generations of students in Loughglynn school and doing such creative projects as choreographing the dance scenes for John McGahern's 'Amongst Women.'

Over the years I returned to my first love – céilí music and it is my belief that more effort should be made to get young people interested in the traditional dance form.

I also like the modern trends and when the Irish band B*witched hit the headlines, it reminded me of my own time with the Granada Girls.

The funniest moment I had with the girls was the night we were playing in Manchester to a full house. I was on the drums as usual and didn't realise that my seat behind the drum kit was precariously positioned on the platform. Just as I was doing a drum roll, I leaned backwards. Instantly my chair gave way and I disappeared through the back curtains from the bandstand.

Some stars devise grand entrances to get their standing ovations; but my back somersault brought the house down as the rest of the band and the dancers went into hysterics. There was only one person with a red face that night but with the passing years, I too can laugh at the night I disappeared like Houdini off the Manchester stage.

Mildred Beirne is a well-known Roscommon-based music teacher and a former member of the Granada Girls. A native of Carracastle, Co Mayo, the mother of two has been a leading light in the revival of traditional music in Ireland over the past 30 years.

Oscar's Last Stand

Mary O'Connor

THE annual carnival was in full swing in Pentony's field. The 'Seven-a-side' football tournament was nearing the final stages. Murder was predicted between the local rivals Rhode and Ballinabrackey.

These dances were high on the social agenda of the surrounding towns, villages and parishes. They were held in the huge white marquee that stretched a good length of the field and was like a citadel of dreams. It promised romance, but it also was a harbinger of heartbreak and provided many a good ould punch-up.

Frank Carroll had booked the biggest bands in the country and the crowds came on bikes, Honda 50s and the more prosperous lads had cars. Dickie Rock and the Miami were billed for Friday night and Oscar was hell-bent on going. However, there were a few obstacles to surmount before that ambition could be realised. The admission fee was certainly out of his reach in light of his current situation. He had just been fired from the local factory the previous week over what he considered a 'thing-of-nothing.'

His job was to put the shoes into the boxes. He was working away as usual when the gaffer came around and called him to the office. He held an open shoe box in his hand. "Malley," he screamed, "what is wrong with that?" Oscar looked at the box, stared at the gaffer and replied: "One black and one brown."

"Exactly," the gaffer shouted. "You're fired. Now get out." The following Friday night Oscar clocked the gaffer in the toilet of the local pub; an incident which required a visit to the doctor and the dentist. As matters stood Oscar's dole hadn't come through and this was why his financial situation could best be described as precarious.

He knew the girls from Mount Lucas were coming to the dance and Oscar had the reputation of being a good dancer. He knew he had impressed Gladys the time he met her in Flanagan's Hall. He had swirled her around to the music of The Black Aces and was doing well until Tom

Feely repaid an old score with an unmerciful 'clatter' and Oscar was left with no alternative but to reciprocate. The result was immediate ejection and a barring order.

He also knew that Bobby Cannon would be coming over from Robertstown. Bobby was a barman, a position that gave him special status in the opinion of the girls, particularly Gladys. Cannon was always flush. His arrival in town dripped of Hollywood; he was the proud owner of a powerful motor-bike, a first cousin to a 'Harley Davidson' and he wore black leathers. His entrance to the pub was always dramatic and he was invariably given VIP treatment. When Bobby removed the leathers down in the gents he emerged in a black tuxedo and his jet-black curly hair shone with a generous application of Brylcreem. He oozed charm and personality and commenced the night's proceedings with a few 'G and Ts.'

Oscar on the other hand was on his last chance in the pub. "Howya Oscar?" Matt, the publican, enquired. "I'm as near the door as the latch," he replied. "You never said a truer word," muttered Matt.

By Friday night Oscar hadn't a tosser and had to resort to 'tick.' "Give us a pint till next week," said Oscar. "You've a calf at grass here, Oscar," said the publican, adding: "It will shortly be ready for the mart."

Just then, Byrne's hackney car from Daingean pulled up with Gladys and her friends. Oscar saw Gladys had her hair done in the bee-hive style and wore a tank-top t-shirt and a gingham skirt that billowed with about four underskirts.

Cannon beamed at Gladys, took her hand and kissed her finger. She blushed. "Give the lady a drink," he ordered, and she was duly delivered with a glass of Britvic orange juice.

Oscar decided to go down to the carnival field and survey the marquee to see if there was some way he could get in for free. He knew there was a strong security system in place. Frankie Carroll hadn't come down in the last shower but Oscar concocted a plan.

With his last few bob he decided to bet on Ballinabrackey. Joe Dunne told him they would beat Rhode. If they did, he might make the price of the dance. But Rhode led all the way and Tim Murphy and the boys were singing the praises of the great fullback Paddy McCormack by singing: 'Gloryo McCormack you're a hero. Gloryo McCormack you're a star.'

Oscar was 'down the Swanee' and reminded himself to clock Dunne the next time he saw him. He walked around the marquee on a 'recce', and wondered if he could slither in if he managed to loosen a tie and move the peg.

"I hope you're not planning anything, Oscar," a voice said. He looked up and saw Big Jack Jones, with hands like shovels stretching out to grab him by the shoulders. Jack was the official 'chucker out' for the carnival dances and watched everyone like a hawk.

By now crowds were thronging in. Gladys and her friends had entered and Cannon was jiving in his tux and Italian patent shoes. Dickie was singing: 'There's always me.' Paddy Mallen came out for a smoke and informed Oscar that Cannon was waltzing with Gladys. "Waltzing very close," he said mischievously, stressing the last two words to annoy him.

Just then Oscar copped Rasher and Dandy approaching, each carrying a thick brown paper bag containing a half-dozen Guinness. They'd had a row the previous week over Dolly, although they made up the next day. He felt it would be easy to get them going again.

"You were doing well with Dolly in the back row at the pictures last night," he said nonchalantly to Rasher.

Dandy hit Rasher an unmerciful box and the half dozen Guinness fell into smithereens. Big Jack Jones came out to intervene as a few more got involved. Then all hell broke loose.

Oscar took advantage of the golden opportunity. As he made a bee-line for inside, Mallen looked at him with a smirk on his face. "Someone might tell Big Jack you didn't pay," he said threateningly.

Oscar fumbled inside his 'mac' and produced the starting handle of a car. "If they do, they'll have to answer to this fella," he grinned, shoving the metal weapon into Mallen's face.

He walked in to the strains of 'Come Back To Stay' thinking how apt the song was for his predicament. He felt his mojo return after the sacking and now no one was going to stop him dancing with Gladys... particularly not that creep Cannon who for all his fine clothes and showing off, wouldn't hold a candle to him when it came to dancing – or fighting.

Mary O'Connor lives in Edenderry, Co Offaly. A well-known writer and historian, she is currently revising her PhD thesis.

38

Some Enchanted Evening In Rockcorry

Patricia Cavanagh

ON a warm Easter Monday evening in 1973 I met the love of my life in our local 'Ballroom of Romance' – the Maple Ballroom in Rockcorry, Co Monaghan. We were dancing to The Swarbrigg brothers and the Times.

Earlier in the evening my friends and I had hitched a lift to the dance from Monaghan town. We were all nurses in the local St Davnet's Psychiatric Hospital and every evening when there was a dance in 'Rock,' the girls got all dolled-up in the nurses home and headed out through Old Cross Square onto the Cootehill Road.

As Patrick Kavanagh put it in his poem, as they were going to Billy Brennan's Barn for a dance: "The bicycles go by in twos and threes..."

In our case it was the girls were going out in twos and threes making our way and hoping to get a lift to the venue.

It was seldom we ever worried about a lift home as normally one of our bunch managed to meet someone with a car and the poor unsuspecting driver got more than he bargained for. A case of all for one and one for all!

There was something about that night as we danced around the hall with its brightly coloured bulbs giving an atmosphere of warmth and romance. Even sipping our orange and eating our Club Milks on the balcony, I could sense the special feeling attached to this dance. My friends were delighted I had met a fella as it meant they didn't have to worry from an early stage about a lift. No wonder I got so many thumbs up from them as I sat beside him.

As the band played out their final songs my new beau, Peter and I, continued to chat. He told me that he also had travelled in a severely overloaded car and there was going to be no lift home for anyone.

I had to make a hasty retreat to my friends, to explain that we should get on the road early – otherwise we might end up walking all the way back to Monaghan.

In the haste to organise ourselves, I didn't make a date to meet up again. Weeks went by and all those thoughts about that night being something different seemed mistaken.

About a month had elapsed before I decided to attend the Ballroom of Romance again. No sooner had we paid in and spruced ourselves up than I felt a hand in mine.

When I looked up, it was Peter smiling. He had got to me before the surge across the floor.

We looked at each other and once again I felt the special chemistry clicking again. "I have my own car tonight," he whispered.

I've never had to worry about getting home since – because Peter and I have been together for over 40 years since that night.

Patricia Cavanagh is a native of Tydavnet, Co Monaghan and is married with three children. A retired psychiatric nurse, her hobbies include photography, creative writing, cycling and swimming.

39

A 'Welcome Home' From Kelley On My First Date

Simon Rickard

IRELAND represented freedom for two weeks every year – the last week of July and the first one of |August.

Like thousands of other children who were sons or daughters of Irish parents exiled in Britain, we made the pilgrimage every summer in the sixties from our home in St Albans outside London to the Irish midlands in our Vauxhall car on the Holyhead to Dublin ferry.

I couldn't wait to land at my Aunt's house because for me the rules changed for that fortnight. My mother, God rest her, was the typical Irish mother in England determined that her son would turn out both well-mannered and hard-working. It meant that I seldom got the freedom to go out with my classmates and enjoy myself.

In Ireland and in the domain of my cousins, I was led on a merry dance of mischief away from my mother's influence. I can't tell you how much I enjoyed it all!

My high-summer rebellion consisted of smoking cigarettes, drinking from the odd flagon of cider and gambling at the toss-pits. And all before we had hit puberty. What more could a boy seeking to become a man want?

We also played a lot of soccer on the Green Field outside the house where being from London and possessing an English accent gave me a certain street cred. My dad brought me to the occasional big match and the lads were in awe of playing with someone who had actually witnessed George Best, Don Givens, Jimmy Greaves and Franny Lee playing in the flesh.

Then one year when the hormones clicked in, we left the football behind us and moved on up the ladder to girls, dates and dances. My two cousins and a friend from next door would look at which showbands were playing to decide our weekend itinerary. Legally we were too young to be going to grown-up dances but no one ever told us.

The one problem was having sufficient money to carry out our plans. I think the dances cost 7/6 to ten shillings at the time. At a stretch it was tough for most young people to rise to such an amount once a week but in our case, we were aiming to go at least twice.

While I had saved up back in England for the homecoming, that money seemed to evaporate in the first few days. It was a case of one for all and all for one. In that short window of time, I was the one with the money and everything was fine until it ran out.

Luckily my two cousins were good gamblers and I still marvel at how they could win at cards and at pitch 'n toss.

They always seemed to accumulate enough so that we could pay for the cost of the trip in a minibus to the venue in the next town, the admission fee and the pocket money required for chips afterwards.

My first memory of the inside of a ballroom was the Central in Tullamore. We walked up the main street, turned right down a slope for about 100 yards where cars were parked and then queued at the door where I was unnerved by the threatening glare of the two bouncers standing on either side.

By the time I got to the hatch to hand over the money and get my ticket, the shirt was stuck to my back in sweat. There was a further set of doors to the inner sanctum and when it was opened, the sound deafened my ears. We had arrived at our musical Nirvana just before midnight and the main band were already giving it socks to make an impression during their first set.

My two cousins were more extroverted than their friend so it suited me to hang around with him. They had already crossed the floor to stick their hands out and both had got fine-looking girls to jive with them.

As I watched from the back wall of the dance hall, I marveled at how anyone could make conversation in such loud surroundings. I admit that I also found the midland accent hard to understand. In fact I was convinced when I first arrived that my grandfather was speaking in the Irish language because I couldn't grasp a word he said.

Later, as my ear got trained, I could hold fleeting conversations with him and more often than not ended up guessing what he had said by responding: "Okay Granddad, catch up later, I'm off down the town now."

It led to the old man asking my mother if I was a simpleton of sorts. Deeply wounded by any such aspersion on her pride and joy, she told him that I was the best at English in my class.

"Well, that's good to hear," he responded, "but I was getting worried that every morning when I asked him did he sleep well, he says he's heading down the town.

I now found myself in a similar predicament when my fried stopped the prettiest girl in the town at the dance, told her who I was and excused himself. He was setting me up with her but I wasn't sure what to do next.

Eventually she led me out onto the floor. She then said something with a big smile and it was like I was talking to my granddad again. "What was I to do?"

I gave her the thumbs up and bluffed a big smile as if to tell her I agreed with her statement. This immediately brought about a disapproving look on her face. I began to panic.

"Did you say that the band is good tonight, because that was why I was giving you the thumbs up sign."

I could see the look of relief on her face. "No I asked you if you were a dab hand with the girls and I thought you were very cocky with your response."

She laughed and so did I, with relief.

"Look," she said at the end of the set, "your friend is calling you up to the front of the stage. Do you want to go on your own?"

"I'd love you to come with me," I said, "but is it ok if we only talk during the breaks?"

She squeezed my hand and gave me a quick kiss on the lips. Then she directed my arm over her shoulder and we walked up the floor to the bandstand area – we were now a couple.

How could my friend or indeed my two cousins better that? There I was arm-in-arm with the most desirable girl in the town and they were looking enviously at me.

"You've wiped all our eyes tonight," said my friend, with a thumbs up gesture just like the one I had used earlier.

As the slow set commenced with Roly Daniels singing, the blonde girl who was the lead female singer with the Nevada smiled across in our direction.

I had already begun a journey into my first smooch under the stage area but was gob-smacked as Kelley – the singer – gestured to my younger cousin to join her for a dance on stage.

He was a little shy at first but then she held her hands out to him and up he jumped and instead of a slow dance – he was a little smaller than she was – she did a version of a slow jive which I can remember to this day.

At the end of the set, she came over and said hello to us all. When she heard my English accent as I was introduced, her remark was – "it's lovely to have you home."

What a night. I had met my first girlfriend and almost immediately afterwards a famous star of the stage had just given me a personal welcome to the land of my forebears.

Life simply couldn't ever get much better than that.

Simon Rickard is the son of Irish parents who has lived all his life in St Albans, England. He still travels regularly to Ireland and in particular to his parents native county of Offaly.

A 'Day' That Lasted A Lifetime

Steve Roche

O URS was a holiday romance that should never have been. We met at a dance neither Joan nor myself had any intention of attending. In reality, we were there because other people needed us to go for their sakes.

Joan was home from the US where she was living in Boston with her aunt and wanted a bit of peace and quiet on her first weekend back in Kanturk.

I was in Manchester working on the pipelines and when I got the few summer weeks off headed back to Ireland for rest and rehabilitation.

Naturally I was delighted to meet up with my pals from Rockchapel on the Cork-Kerry border but was less than enamoured when they told me they wanted to head to the dance hall on my first night home.

I tried to talk them out of it but they were all mad to see Muriel Day singing. A short time earlier that year (1969), she had represented Ireland in the Eurovision Song Contest with 'The Wages of Love'. She was the first woman to represent Ireland and the song finished a creditable seventh.

Of course, the lads knew I had an Anglia de Luxe which I had bought the previous year and now had it back on the road again. They wanted me to drive them to the Edel Quinn Hall in Kanturk and weren't taking 'no' for an answer.

Joan was still suffering from jet lag and would not have ventured out... except her younger sister begged her to go.

She said that her mother wouldn't let her out alone but everything would be ok if Joan tagged along.

We were both reluctant dancers that night and our chance encounter would change our lives forever. We met across that crowded ballroom and it certainly proved an enchanted evening.

We hit it off so well from the start, and with three weeks off, I offered to drive her around while she was at home. Not everyone had a car in the sixties and it was a way for me to be with her as much as possible.

Cars in those day were nowhere near as reliable as they are now and I suppose mine had been idle for a while which didn't help. You can imagine my embarrassment and her concern when the car broke down on a country road near Mallow in the dead of night.

I could see an understandable flicker of concern on her face but I assured that I would get her home soon. I gave the old vehicle a five-minute break and then poured a pint of oil into it, hoping that it would do the business. Fortunately, the engine purred when I turned the ignition and Joan saw there had been no ulterior motive on my part.

Those days and nights we spent together flew, culminating in the two of us dancing the night away at the Majestic Ballroom. I was seldom at home and I think Joan's mother was none too happy that every time she looked around, I was whisking her daughter away in my Anglia.

Still, I have a lot to thank that woman for. When we went back to the real world, I returned to Manchester and very soon was relocated to Birmingham working on the pipeline. Joan, meanwhile, was finding it difficult to settle back in America.

It was tough being apart but we kept writing to each other every week and I looked forward to receiving her letters.

During the holidays, her mother and I had got on well; I think she knew I was serious about her daughter from the off. One day later that year she was reading the Examiner and saw an advertisement looking for IBM computer operators in the National Westminster Bank in Birmingham. Seemingly, all the accounts were being centralised there and they were looking for experienced personnel.

Joan had a background in that area and I can't tell you how delighted both of us were when she was one of the people who got a job offer. We got engaged that same year and once she was living in Birmingham, we set a date and got married in 1971.

Due to the nature of my job, we were on the move soon again – this time to North Wales where we lived happily until the early eighties. Then we made the big decision and decided to come home to live in Ireland.

We have lived in Kanturk ever since with our family and our lives have been blessed. And all because the most unlikely holiday romance got the chance to flourish the night Muriel Day and the Dave Glover Showband played in the local dancehall.

It was a Day in our lives that has lasted forever.

Steve Roche is a native of Rockchapel, Co Cork and is married to Joan with three grown-up children. His hobbies are writing songs and stories about his travels.

Thumbing
To Paradise

Maura Flynn

WE would position ourselves on the road about seven o'clock with thumbs out to every car that passed. It was important to start early, as not everyone would give a lift to two teenage girls standing at the side of the road with a hopeful look on their faces. Also there were not that many cars on the road in rural Ireland in the 1960s.

Sometimes an hour would pass between cars, but we never gave up hope, we were determined to get to Pontoon Ballroom to see our favourite Showbands. My friend Chris and I had absolutely no idea how we would get home, the important thing was to get there. We lived about an hour from Pontoon, so getting a taxi was out of the question, and anyway our funds would not have stretched that far.

We were lucky hitchers and nearly always met somebody who would be passing our way. On the odd occasion when our luck ran out we had an old reliable to count on. Mickey was a middle-aged man with a Morris Minor who had a 'thing' for Chris, and if the worst came to the worst she would have the last dance with Mickey and guarantee our lift home. I would be warned to say I was spending the night at her house, so we both got out of the car together and she would avoid further amorous advances. Oh, the cruelty of teenagers.

Micky's hopes were dashed every time, but he never gave up, and could always be relied on as a last resort. In later years my friend's sister, Mary, got married to a man with a car. Tom and Mary lived next door to me, and they were kind enough to bring us to see the Showbands. I remember especially one night we went to see the Royal in the Royal Ballroom in Castlebar, and Tom bought me my first alcoholic drink. It was a Babycham, in a stemmed glass with a picture of a fawn on the side. With the bubbles tickling my nose I felt so grown up and sophisticated.

My uncle Brendan always went to the Royal Ballroom and taught me all the steps of the quickstep, foxtrot and the old-time-waltz. We went regularly to the Pavilion Ballroom in Westport on St. Stephen's night. All the lads arrived home from England for Christmas and they stood out a mile with their drainpipe trousers and winkle-picker shoes. They had all the latest moves too and taught us how to jive and do the twist.

The girls wanted to dance with those lads and often a fight broke out among the locals over some girl or other. If you were lucky, the lad you fancied would ask you to go to the mineral bar for a bottle of orange and a packet of custard creams.

Another time when I was going out with this nice fella I missed my lift home. We had to spend the night in his granny's house. She was an elderly lady and we were terrified she would come down the stairs and find us. So we spent the whole night sitting bolt upright on her sitting-room couch, and jumping at every creak that old house made.

I got the first bus home the next morning, all the while racking my brains as to what I would tell my parents. I was saved by the most unexpected source – the sudden arrival of my uncle and family from America.

The whole house was upside down and in the bedlam I managed to sneak upstairs unnoticed. For the only time in my life, I was delighted to hear my mother shout: "Are you going to sleep all day or what! Get up and give a hand or the Yanks will be here."

And as for the lad I spent the night sitting beside in his Granny's –well, we are still together 51 years later.

Maura Flynn resides in Westport and is now retired. She is a member of the Ward9 writers group and her hobbies include baking and reading.

Following The Wrong Car Home

Eileen Ludlow

S OME of us followed the bands, others were devoted to particular venues. Either way Sunday nights were the highlight of the week back in those days of our youth.

Getting to a venue when you lived in the country was a big deal as there were few cars and securing a lift was crucial for the week's main dancing night. Sometimes it was necessary to tell white lies at home about the transport you had arranged, even if you hadn't – just to keep your parents happy.

They preferred if you were in safe hands with Mary Joe who would not exceed 30mph, instead of Mick the Madman with his souped-up Anglia.

Preparations for a dance could begin as early as a Tuesday or Wednesday as we hit Cassidy's fabric shop in Cork's Patrick St. We were forever looking for a lucky outfit which if you had scored, then it might get another outing.

This was the era of the mini-skirt, responsible for the break down of good society and the root cause of scandal, according to the clergy. An elderly parishioner was chatting to his neighbour one Sunday after Mass, when the irate PP approached, bristling with anger about the "hussy" who he said came to Mass "without her skirt."

Tom took a long puff of his pipe, put his 84-year-old head to one side and said: "Anything that makes an old man feel young again can't be a bad thing, Father". The priest had no answer to that.

The material purchased was no good until it was transformed into the perfect outfit. This was done with the help of borrowed patterns and my grandmother's sewing machine.

For the good of my parents a longer skirt was put on over the "hussy" model and the extra clothing was deposited at a friend's house to be collected en route home.

Sunday was a full day with Mass first, then a match to play or attend… and then on to the long awaited dance.

Away I went to the sound of "make sure you are home at a decent hour" or "what in God's name are you wearing?" (If only they knew).

One particularly dark and foggy night, we all piled into Mary's Morris Minor, three in the front and four in the back – all girls.

The fun had begun. Kathleen had her hair backcombed and so elevated that she had to share a front seat as her hair wouldn't fit in the back. She carried a knitting needle to uplift her style should it be needed. This also served as a weapon if a stray hand landed in the wrong place on the dance floor. She later became a nun, so maybe the knitting needle was part of the armoury of a would be religious sister.

There was Joan, shy and sweet-natured but had the lads fighting for her attention.

We arrived in Enniskeane full of anticipation. It was about 10.30 and the big band was due on at 11pm. After paying in, it was into the ladies room to check our appearance before emerging into the hall.

Helen, one of our crew had a date, a cheapskate who always met her inside, ensuring that she paid her own way in.

On this particular night the band were The Smokey Mountain Ramblers who had a big following. That night I met up with someone I had my eye on for a while – good-looking but boy did he know it? He could dance but after a mineral with him, I'd no aspiration to stay in his company.

Afterwards, as we all filed out into the damp murky night, we could hardly find the car in the worsening fog. It was swirling like something from a horror movie. How would we get home in such weather, we wondered?

Then a VW Beetle passed us and our driver identified it as a neighbour. We decided to use it to guide ourselves the 20 or so miles home. Chat about the night kept us going and we didn't notice time passing. Mary suddenly asked the time as the car in front pulled up in someone's farmyard.

We had followed the wrong car and actually discovered that we had gone in the wrong direction and were now 40 miles from home with not a huge amount of petrol left on board.

The other driver gave us directions after admitting he had found it strange to see the lights behind him follow him all the way into his own yard.

Our poor driver was cross-eyed by the time we eventually made it home nearing dawn. I sneaked in and managed to silence the dogs and tiptoed to my room where I fell over the little Jack Russell. I grabbed a coat to steady myself which brought the hall stand crashing down.

There was a thundering roar from the parents and a "what time is this to get home?"

I thought I would be grounded for life by my parents but the days passed and by the following Sunday we were off dancing again.

Eileen Ludlow is from Farran, Co Cork and has lived in Drumconrath, Co Meath for over 40 years. She is married to Peter and has three grown-up children and five grandchildren. Her hobbies include reading, gardening, painting and writing stories from life's events.

43

Catching The Wave

David Fegan

THERE was much to commend my parents' sense of timing my conception, whereby my teenage years exactly spanned the interval from summer of 1955 to summer of 1962. After all, this window of time beautifully encapsulated the rock and roll era, as a new and vibrant cultural revolution emerged.

For teenagers growing up in Ireland, the emergence of rock and roll was synonymous with first hearing on Radio Éireann, the likes of Bill Haley, Elvis Presley, Jerry Lee Lewis, Chuck Berry, Fats Domino, Little Richard, Buddy Holly, the Everley Brothers and others.

So, tuning in to radio and catching the broadcast wave was really the only way to be part of this novel cultural experience.

Which particular musical tracks teenagers might happen to hear however, was simply a matter of serendipity or random chance. In the pre-TV fifties, the wireless was central to domestic entertainment but what was heard on it was fairly stringently determined by adults, in particular by parents. Teenagers opportunities for hearing rock and roll were therefore quite limited. Somewhat exceptionally, a programme such as 'Hospital's requests' offered possibilities of hearing folk music, skiffle and rock and roll, played for the benefit of some lucky patients.

It was not until October 1962 that Radio Éireann commenced broadcasting 'Ireland's Top 10'. During the 1950s, however, listeners living in northern or eastern seaboard counties could pick up BBC Light programme wireless transmissions especially if they had an outdoor antenna.

Also civilian audiences could sometimes tune in to transmissions from the American Forces Network in Europe (AFN), since American music was very popular but rarely played by most European broadcasting stations.

By far the most popular station with Irish teenagers of that era was Radio Luxembourg. A large portion of 208's output was confined to early evening 15 or 30 minute commercial slots, frequently employed by specific record companies (labels) such as Decca, Pye, Phillips, London American and others, with the specific aim of promoting the very latest singles from the labels in question.

My personal favourite broadcast was Jack Jackson's Jukebox Show but the station had other top DJs such as Jimmy Young, Alan Freeman and Pete Murray.

I grew up in a house possessing a fine floor-standing Pye radiogram incorporating 11 independent tuning wavebands. It also had the capability of reproducing quality sound from 7-inch singles, from 10 and 12 inch long-playing vinyl discs (LPs) and moderate sound from old-fashioned 78 rpm shellac records.

It was a family utility and consequently had to be shared. To own a personal portable radio was financially out of the question. The invention of the transistor revolutionised electronics over the next quarter century. Traditional bulky, power-hungry lifetime-limited vacuum tubes were replaced by new solid state devices which were extremely compact, exhibited remarkably low power consumption and were fabricated by specialised techniques, from very pure forms of Germanium or Silicon.

Towards the end of the fifties, European manufacturers realised the potential of the vast market of teenagers seeking to own personal portable transistorised radios (trannies) at affordable prices. They responded with innovative products.

Summertime jobs in Dublin were sparse and paid little.

Serendipitously, the summer of 1960 was pre-Leaving certificate and I was offered a job working in England with the UK Construction and Engineering Company, which I gratefully accepted.

For a 17-year-old, it was most certainly not an easy sojourn in a foreign land – working in Oxfordshire with a gang of mainly hardened Irish navvies, contracted to lay a 24-inch diameter gas pipeline through many miles of predominantly rural landscape. Since the nature of the contract demanded seven working days per week, there was precious little opportunity for socialising or for days off.

I had certain delegated responsibilities, most important of which was group tea-boy. Drinking water was sourced by me from which buckets were then filled and carried manually back to wherever the gang happened to be working. Morning tea-break was the most demanding, hang-overs slowly dispersed as cigarettes were quietly smoked. Egos were not to be tampered with under any circumstances.

I was also responsible for the provision of clandestine showering facilities, often rapidly constructed, on-the-go in pop-up fashion, since the long summer days were frequently blisteringly hot, and hygiene mattered.

Camaraderie was wonderful, working with lads from all over Ireland and there were many acts of bravura and foolhardiness as the sweaty band of buccaneers menacingly advanced on Oxford, the city of dreaming spires or should that be the city of aspiring dreams?

Ten weeks of contract flashed rapidly by, but whatever free time I had was made infinitely more interesting by virtue of having made the pilgrimage to the best audio shop in Oxford, just as soon as savings reached the purchasing threshold level of a Braun T3 receiver. What a thrill!

An immediate consequence of this purchase was the ability to maintain closer contact with home, via Radio Éireann's medium wave transmissions, detectable at reasonable levels of signal fidelity, especially in late evening.

After a day's intensive work it was such a relaxing experience to recline in meadowland and visually explore the constellations, while listening to some of the latest music from back home, by new artistes such as Brendan, Dickie, Butch, Joe, Red et al. (so much our own that we referred to them on a first name basis). Gradually musical careers were becoming established as part of what became the showband scene.

The Braun T3 receiver accompanied me for almost a quarter of a century until it finally ceased operation in 1983. It was the most valuable piece of audio equipment I ever invested in, the pleasures gained far exceeding the monetary cost. However, it's ultimate Sony replacement (ICF-SW100) still catches the wave exceedingly well so what more can one ask for?

Who needs internet, Wi-Fi, podcasting, streaming, subscription services, and DAB (digital audio broadcasts) with the inevitable dropouts? Better to get a life, get a portable chip/transistor wireless! Catch the real broadcast wave!

David Fegan is a Research Scientist and Emeritus Professor of High Energy Astrophysics at UCD. A native of Dublin, his hobbies include hill walking and problem solving and likes to spend quality time in Wexford.

44

Marching To
The Same Beat

Cathal Gunning

JOHNNY, the drummer previously known as Maurice, was watching. On stage a dynamo, his hands a blur moving over the snare, the hi-hats, the bass and the tom-toms. Up there, he was sanctified. "Wrists on your man going ninety, he's something else"

Away from the stage Johnny was tired, a beat out of step with life. He propped himself on one leg, eyes moving from his coffee mug to the gathering dusk. The scent – perspiration vs. Old Spice – strong, the night's cold not jiving with his too-tight collar. Inside, the dancehall sang out with excitement, but Johnny was spent. He thought of Mary, at home alone.

Johnny clicked his fingers, trying for the timing of 'Fun, Fun, Fun'. Inside the hall, sticks bounced off the skins a half-second faster than his fingers clicked, enough to throw the tune. His frustration distracted when two girls sashayed past. Both in tight skirts, high hemlines. Skirts got shorter, nights got longer, he thought. Both were busy rationing an almost-empty pack of cigarettes to notice Johnny, half-asleep standing there. He watched them chatting.

A short distance away a lad hopped off his bicycle and propped it against the fence. Johnny thought he recognised him. He observed how the kid tapped a hand to his chest in time with music on the air, the other clapping off his thigh. He recognised the choreography of rhythm, of drumming.

Johnny smiled. He almost laughed when he saw the kid freeze, awkward, when he noticed the girls. Two faces lit up. The first girl happy to see him, half-decent at hiding it; the lad delighted to see her, useless at hiding it. He tried to switch to serious cool. Her friend wasn't happy to see him and wasn't arsed pretending.

The kid was a boy trying hard to morph into someone older. He spoke to the first girl in a drumfire palpitation of words and she replied in kind.

Her friend tugged her sleeve and gestured to the dancehall, saying: "The sixth-year lads are all inside".

That lad, Johnny thought. Didn't he work with that same girl in the newsagents at weekends? The two of them as awkward behind the counter as they were tonight!

That lad could have been himself. Could have been Johnny when he was still known as Maurice, standing outside the parochial hall shaking, nervous and cold, after his first show. Back when his sticks would slip from sweating hands, when he still said "Maurice" if asked his name.

* * *

She wanted a light and for her troubles, she got lukewarm Club Orange spilled over her dress, a dark stain mapped against bright pink. She too had a friend, caught between laughter and reproach. Maurice, embarrassed, stammering an apology. Hand poised but afraid to help.

And Mary surprised him, dress ruined yet she laughed. The sound was musical, beautiful and edged with mischief. That flash of white teeth, flick of black hair, the hand clapped to her mouth. And then she took his outstretched hand. Her friend gone to tell the lads: "Look what your man's after doing to Mary's dress".

"You play the drums, right?"

"I, yeah, I mean, yeah."

And she was saying: "You'd want steadier hands than that."

"I was distracted."

"Is that so? What by?"

"The most beautiful girl in Ireland."

And he was taking the piss if he thought something that corny would work, and if she was laughing with him before, she'd be laughing at him now.

Then that laugh again, that laugh better than any music, that dazzling smile, and: "What's your name?"

"Johnny."

And she asked: "Do you want to go somewhere quieter, Johnny?"

And he did. That night, every night since, Johnny wanted nothing more than to go somewhere quieter with her.

* * *

"Here, lad."

Johnny yelled this out, louder than he'd have wished. "What's your name?"

"Eoin", the lad answered.

Johnny looked him up and down, surveying a potential drummer.

"How'd you spell that?"

"E-O-G-H-A-N"

Hardly rock-n-roll, Johnny thought. A too-large blazer, no doubt borrowed from his brother, baby-blue shirt, half-inch too-short trousers; he looked more holy communion than Surfin' USA.

"Right, three things, Joey," Johnny started.

"It's Eoghan," said the kid.

"Not tonight it isn't," Johnny said. "That's the first thing. The second thing is ditch that jacket."

"I can't, it's my cousins."

"Leave it in the van, get it after the show"

"Third thing's pull up your sleeves. Past the elbow, bunched up like you've big arms, too big for your shirt. Drummers have muscles."

"Drummers?"

"You can play, right?"

Johnny passed him the sticks.

Five minutes later, Johnny pushed Eoghan through the backstage door over half-hearted protests.

"What songs."

"Beach Boys? Whatever they want. What do you listen to?"

Now his ear was pressed against the stage door, crouched out of sight beneath the window. He barely heard the front-man mutter "Johnny, you bollocks," away from the mike before booming: "We've a fresh face on the drums this evening, God love him. Let's have a hand for – What's your name?"

"Joey."

Johnny never heard the rest over the frenzied drum-line of "Darlin'", the chatter of drumbeats leading the way for squawking guitar, shoes tapping to the beat, keeping time. He looked to the road, a winding stretch of cracked tarmac. The long road home, worth it to be with her tonight – somewhere quiet.

Cathal Gunning is a native of Blackrock, Dublin and now shares his time between Dublin and Mayo. His debut novel, 'Innocents', will be published this autumn.

| 45 |

Ballroom Of Romance How Are Ya!

Maeve Edwards

THE date August 12, 1967 is etched in my brain. I'd like to be able to tell you it was because I met the love of my life on that day and have been living in wedded bliss ever since. What a story that would be. But then again, it probably wouldn't be a story at all. As Tolstoy says: "Happy families are all alike, every unhappy family is unhappy in its own way."

But unhappy families are not what this is about. This is about something much less momentous. It is about four young girls, born and bred in a northside Dublin suburb, coming to a ballroom for the first time – The Gleneagle Ballroom, Killarney.

August 12 was a Saturday. It was my friend Mary's eighteenth birthday. We'd promised her we'd go to Killarney to celebrate, and that afternoon the four of us headed confidently for the Naas Dual Carriageway, the Leaving Cert behind us and the world before us.

We paired off, Mary and I standing near the junction of the Long Mile Road, and our two friends moving further past the small clumps of our fellow hitch-hikers. We adjusted our knapsacks, stuck out our thumbs, brandished our "Killarney Please" signs, and before long, we were on our way.

Our destination was the An Oige Youth Hostel in Killarney, and all of us arrived unscathed within an hour of each other. Our evening meal consisted of the sandwiches we'd made earlier in our mothers' kitchens, and then it was time to get ourselves ready for the real event of the day.

Our experience of the opposite sex was zilch. We'd all been to convent schools. We all had younger brothers. We'd also been to the local "hop" where pimply teenagers lurched awkwardly with us during the slow sets; but never had we been to a Ballroom. We had some hazy idea that a ballroom was where real romance began. We were sure of it. Weren't there real men here in the Gleneagle Ballroom? Real Kerry men. Not skinny boys

'Queen of Country and Irish' Margo O'Donnell, sister of singer Daniel O'Donnell, with actor Frank O'Donovan on the set of RTÉ Television's soap opera *The Riordans*, at Dunboyne, County Meath, 20 January, 1969. O'Donovan played the character of Batty Brennan on the show. *Photo by Michael O'Reilly*
See Margo's story, Page 19

The Miami Showband playing to a jubilant crowd in the Television Club, Harcourt Street, Dublin, 27 May, 1968. Pat McCarthy (trombone), Dickie Rock (vocals), Brian McCoy (trumpet), Fran O'Toole (keyboard/vocals) and Paul Ashford (bass). Not shown in this shot: Des McAlea (sax/guitar), Clem Quinn (lead guitar) and Tony Bogan (drums). These were the heady days of the showband era and The Miami were at the top of their game. *Photo by Michael O'Reilly*

The crowd gets their hands on Jimmy Swarbrigg, vocalist with Mullingar showband The Times, at the Television Club, Harcourt Street, Dublin, 14 October, 1968. *Photo by Michael O'Reilly*

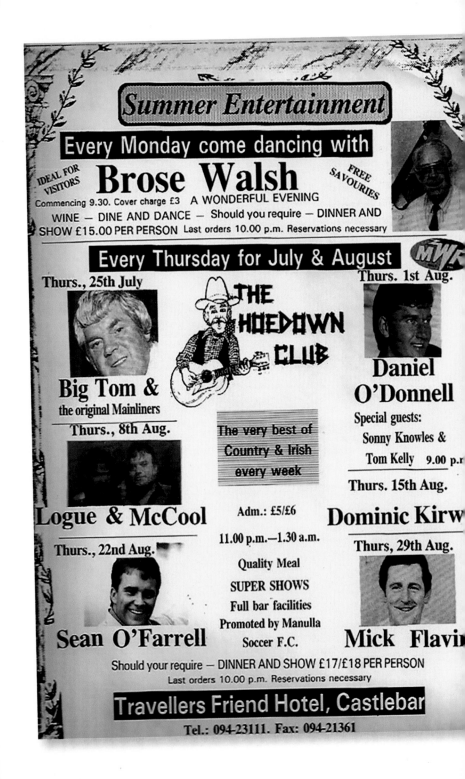

Members of the Brose Walsh Band (below) with former Taoiseach Albert Reynolds. Back row: John Noel Walsh, Brose Walsh, Joe O'Neill and James Walsh. Seated: Tomas Walsh and Jimmy Deacy. Right: a letter from former US President Richard Nixon's wife Patty thanking the group for playing at a function. Left: The band headline the summer entertainment bill at the Travellers Friend Hotel in Castlebar, Co Mayo.

THE WHITE HOUSE

October 14, 1970

Dear Walsh brothers,

I am most appreciative of the part you had in making my visit to Ballinrobe so very interesting and enjoyable.

My stay in Ireland, though brief, was delightful. I shall recall all of you with fondness, for your warmth and hospitality were deeply moving.

With best wishes,

Sincerely,

Patricia Nixon

Walsh Brothers
In Care of Walsh Irish Band
Castlebar
County Mayo, Ireland

Pictured at the Gleneagle
Ballroom, Killarney
last August with her
singing idol, Dickie
Rock, on the occasion of
her 65th birthday was
Rose Hegarty together
with (left to right)
her daughter Donna,
granddaughter Lily Rose
and sister Dolly.
See Story, Page 121

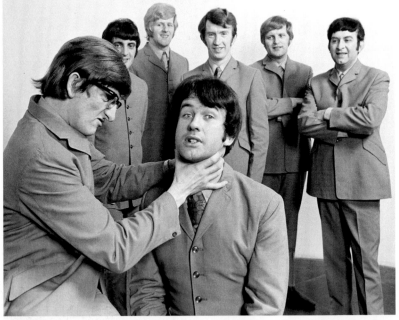

Cork showband The Dixies, Dublin, 25 January, 1969. Drummer Joe
McCarthy gets hold of vocalist Brendan O'Brien's neck, while Theo
Cahill (trombone/sax/flute), Steve Lynch (lead guitar), Finbarr
O'Leary (keyboard), Sean Lucey (sax/clarinet) and
Chris O'Mahoney (bass) stand in the background.
Photo by Michael O'Reilly

Dancehall Days: When Showbands Ruled The Stage
by Michael O'Reilly was published by
Gill & MacMillan in 2014.

from Dublin who fumbled and foostered and couldn't string two words together. What we would do with these real men, we weren't quite sure, but the object was to find one.

We'd heard about the showbands. We'd seen black and white newscasts on RTÉ. We'd heard the kind of music they played. We weren't quite sure if it was our kind of music, but the thrill of seeing uniformed band members moving in unison and belting out the songs was intoxicating. Oh, the headiness of seeing a trumpeter on stage, or a saxophonist down on one knee eking out the sadness of a melody. We could hardly contain ourselves as we pulled on our mini-skirts, slapped on our eyeliner and headed out the Muckross Road.

We could feel rather than see the Gleneagle Ballroom before us in the dimming August night. The whole building was throbbing as we joined the queue and handed over our five shillings. Did we capture a first feeling of uncertainty when one of the doormen sniggered? Was he laughing at us? "Down from Dublin for the showband, are ye, girls? Do ye not think ye'll be out of your league?"

"How did he know we were from Dublin?"

The women in the Ladies cloakroom were crammed together grappling for space at the mirrors. The room was hot and sticky and smelled of talcum powder and roll-on deodorant. Lipstick was being reapplied, eyeliner painted on, rouge smudged into cheek bones. Nobody paid us the slightest attention but all four of us knew that we'd made a big mistake.

Every woman there looked like Jackie Kennedy. They wore twin sets and pearls. They had backcombed hair, and pale pink lips. They wore dirndl skirts and sling back shoes. There wasn't a mini in sight. We were in a time warp. Our big sisters used to dress like this and the last thing we wanted was to look like them. We extricated ourselves and fled for the dance floor area.

A slow set was in progress, and all of us, one after the other, were swept away first by one male, then another, until we were each lost in the maelstrom of bodies, all shuffling together like a large behemoth.

My partner, the one who'd asked me up, put his head on my shoulder. I could feel the sweat of his forehead dampen my dress. He said something, but the noise in the ballroom was thunderous and I shook my head pointing to my ear. Undeterred, he pulled me to him placing his head on my shoulder again. The swarm of bodies was moving in a clockwise direction towards the band area. I could see Dickie Rock. I could hear his words "From the Candy Store ..." He sang as we swept inexorably past. I was miles from where I'd left my friends. Around me, couples necked and clung to each other in a heaving flow of humanity.

I wanted Sergeant Pepper, Norwegian Wood and Marmalade skies. I wanted to laze with The Kinks on a sunny afternoon. I wanted the tinny sound of the record player in our local hop. I wanted to be with boys, not a grown man with Brylcreemed hair, who was trying to place his lips against my neck. I was in the wrong place. This ballroom was not for me.

At the end of the set, my partner muttered "thanks" and was gone. I was left stranded in the top right hand corner and battled my way back. I found Mary in similar dismay to me. "They're too old for us," she confirmed. "Come on, let's find the others and we'll go get a bag of chips."

I'd love to tell you that that was the end of the story, but it wasn't. The following day, we were left stranded on the side of the road, unable to get a hitch back to Dublin. We'd to shamefacedly return to Killarney and plead with the station master to let us on a train bound for Dublin. He insisted on telephoning Mary's father to tell him his daughter was penniless and tearful down in his station. Money was wired down to us, and we returned home, our tails between our legs, our reckless hitchhiking adventure discovered. Ballroom of Romance how are ya!

Maeve Edwards is from Clontarf, Dublin but now lives in Bray, Co Wicklow. A mother of two, her writing has been shortlisted for many awards.

46

Jack The Lad

Tom Aherne

' JACK' is not his real name but he was a member of our group attending dances in the 1970s. He was only an average dancer, but a real charmer with words, who'd ask any girl onto the floor. He liked to take a few drinks but was rarely drunk. I saw girls refusing to dance with him, preferring to dance with pioneers who were in great demand.

As you may have gathered, when Jack was around there were always funny things happening. One night at a neighbouring dance hall Jack arrived in good form. He crossed the floor to where the girls were sitting. He started at the top near the bandstand and proceeded to ask each girl in turn, and despite being steady on the feet, he did not succeed in getting a partner.

What happened next surprised everyone. Jack fell to the floor in front of the girls who surrounded him as he lay prostrate. One of the girls was a nurse and was concerned in case Jack had suffered a heart attack. She knelt down beside him and gave him the kiss of life, which seemed to have little effect, and it went on like this for a good while.

A big crowd gathered around to watch the proceedings. Then once again, to the amazement of everybody, Jack sat up with a smile on his face and said: "Carry on, that was lovely, I haven't got such a kiss in years."

Strangely instead of people being annoyed, he got a round of applause as he got to his feet and he wasn't short of a dancing partner for the rest of the night. He was like a modern day Lazarus, coming back from the dead.

Pushing and shoving to find a dance partner in the marquees often led to crushes which caused people to fall through the tent canvas and onto the ground outside. Jack was a master at getting such a crush started if he thought that girls were slow to dance. Then when patrons ended up on the ground, he would offer his help to get the girls back on their feet and invariably coaxed one out onto the floor away from the crush that he himself had staged.

At another dance, the band was playing a lovely slow waltz but the dancers were shy on getting out onto the floor. Jack was merry and being the character he was, we had a bet with him that he wouldn't cross the floor and ask a girl to dance.

"No problem," said Jack, who turned in my direction and asked: "Will you come with me, Tommy?" There were two new girls there that night and as we walked across, Jack said we would chance our arm with them.

Fortunately, they both agreed to dance and we had the floor to ourselves for a while. However it didn't take too long to see that Jack and his partner were at odds. Next thing she turned on her heels and abandoned Jack out on the empty dance floor.

When I got back after the set ended, I asked Jack what had happened?

According to Jack the master storyteller, the girl put her high heel shoe into the fold of his trouser leg and her foot remained there all around the floor. "She nearly had the trousers pulled off me," he explained. "I had no choice but to tell her to sit down while my modesty was still intact."

That version caused a lot of laughter. In fact, a crowd gathered around as he retold it several times, always adding a little as the story entered a new telling.

Jack emigrated to Australia around the time the Showband era finished and ended up herding cattle in the outback. If the gift of the gab is universal, then I'd say he was a big hit down under and never had any problems getting a partner to dance.

Tom Aherne is a native of Glensharrold Carrigkerry, Co Limerick and he has had a number of articles published over the years. His other hobbies include crafts, local radio, sport, history, dancing, and country music.

47

The Buckled Wheel

Tony McCormack

PADRAIG DALY was a work colleague who told me the delightful dance hall story of how he and his wife Fiona met many years ago.

"I seemed to have just morphed into becoming a farmer. It was tradition at that time that the eldest son would take over the farm. I left school at fifteen to begin working the land full-time.

I dedicated much of my twenties to building it up and taking care of my elderly parents. They both died within a year of each other, leaving me with an empty house and four bedrooms to fill. A quicker-than-anticipated receding hairline hastened my search for a partner so I wandered out to the local pubs and dancehalls in search of a suitable match.

Back then the best place to meet your future spouse was in the dancehalls. We met up in the local pub, had a few pints before going on bikes to the dance. The journey to the nearest hall was about twelve miles but we thought nothing of cycling twice that distance.

At every crossroads more people joined our lovelorn peloton – all united with the common goal of finding love.

At the dancehall, my sense of anticipation never weaned despite my low success rate. My initial three years of searching didn't bear much result. Then, one Sunday night in early June 1955, I saw one particular girl. Most nights you would know virtually everybody in the hall, but she was a stranger to my eyes.

I approached her, stuttered out a few words that included 'dance' and 'please' and with a smile, she accepted my offer. Over the next few hours, we danced, drank minerals and exchanged details of our backgrounds. Most importantly I got a promise that she would meet me the following Sunday night.

I went home ecstatic knowing that the girl that I had just met – Fiona Kelly – was very special.

The following morning there was a spring in my step. I counted down each waking hour to the next dance.

As bad luck would have it, I was cycling on my own that Sunday night and hit a bump on the road that buckled the front wheel. I was stuck in the middle of nowhere and not one person came along the road to give me a lift. After trying for an hour I had to accept my faith and push the bike home with a heavy heart.

The following days were hell. I practiced my apology to Fiona a million times. All I could imagine was her sitting at the corner of the dancehall and watching the door for me to come in.

Worse still was the torture in my head at the thoughts of someone else dancing with her. The following Sunday, I borrowed a neighbour's bike and started out an hour earlier just in case the same thing happened again. When I got to the dance there was no sign of her, she never turned up. I had only seen her once before so she might be a visitor. For the next couple of weeks I broadened my search to a number of other dance halls but to no avail.

A few weeks afterwards I was in Carrick-on-Shannon shopping and getting my bike wheel fixed. To my astonishment, one of Fiona's friends was working in the premises. I introduced myself and explained what had happened and was delighted to have the offending wheel in my hand as evidence. She explained that Fiona was working in London but would be home for Christmas. She agreed to contact her to give her my version of the story. The outcome was that I found out Fiona would be in the ballroom on the first Saturday after Christmas and that she would meet me.

The whole meaning of Christmas day passed me by that year, as it was all about my redemption date. It was a frosty night that Saturday but wild horses would not have stopped me from getting to the dancehall. I got there about two hours early. Fiona accepted my apology and we met another three times before she returned to London.

She was from the neighbouring parish and had been living abroad for a number of years. She was considering moving home and was in the process of applying for work.

That Christmas she managed to get a job. Our courtship was short as we both knew what we wanted and realised that time was not on our side. We got married with the usual goals and dreams that most couples have when starting their lives together. Over 50 years of marriage, three children and six grandchildren later, we still fondly recall the famous bike and dancehall story."

For the record, Pádraig and Fiona were just shy of celebrating their 60th wedding anniversary when they both passed to their eternal reward within weeks of each other last year.

Tony McCormack is from Delvin, Co Westmeath. Married with two children, he is a development officer with Westmeath Community Development and is a part-time farmer.

Thumbing When
The Chips Were Down

Rosemary McDermott

WHEN I see the revival of country music and jiving these days, it takes me back over 40 years. Oh, those heady days of travelling to dances in the ballrooms.

One night as my friend, Anne, and I were in my bedroom listening to pop music on the radio, my glammed-up older sister, Celine, and her equally glamorous friend, Kate, came in. As our eyes widened in admiration, I asked. "Where are you two going tonight?"

"We're going to see The Indians," Kate told us excitedly. "They're great, why don't you and Anne come with us?"

"We'd love to," I said. "But I doubt Mammy and Daddy would allow me."

"Ask your parents, Anne," Celine suggested. Then turning to me, she went on: "Talk nicely to Mammy and Daddy, they might let you go, especially as you'd be with us."

After a lot of pleading, both sets of parents gave in and we were on our way to our first real dance, which was in the Borderland Ballroom in Muff, County Donegal.

Once we got the taste, there was no stopping us. Normally we had no transport so we'd have to thumb a lift and we were never disappointed – until one night when our luck appeared finally to run out.

We were getting ready to go to a dance in The Castle Ballroom, in Dungiven.

"You should be staying at home tonight," said my mother. "It's going to snow."

"Don't worry, Mammy, we'll have no bother getting a lift," Celine said.

We got a lift almost immediately with a couple who were also going to the dance. As we made our way into The Castle, they told us that we could get back home with them if we wanted.

We had a fantastic night and when the dance was over, I dallied after we collected the coats from the cloakroom. "I'll nip into the ladies before we go," I said. Inside I took a comb from my handbag, and began to backcomb my hair. The girls in the end had to come looking for me because I took so long.

Celine was exasperated. "We better get a move on."

"Just a minute," I smiled mischievously as I finished my coiffure work. "You wouldn't know who we might run into outside," I said, mindful that I'd had a few dances with a fellow from Strabane earlier.

"Gosh, it's snowed heavily all night," Anne remarked, when she spotted the white carpet outside. We hurried towards the car park but our hearts sank when we saw that the couple's car was no longer there.

"Now look what you've done, those people have left without us." Celine shrieked.

I felt really guilty. We were stranded in the middle of a snowfall with miles to go before we'd sleep. Crestfallen, we sat on a window-sill in Dungiven Main St. Anne, her teeth chattering from the cold, sobbed: "What are we going to do?"

Tears flowed. Sitting shivering on the sill, we heard the sound of an engine. As it trundled slowly up the street towards us, we were relieved to see that its indicator had come on. A fish and chip van pulled up beside us and the driver called out. "Where are you going to?"

"We're going in the Strabane direction," Celine shouted back.

"Ah, you're in luck," the driver said cheerfully. "We're going up to Strabane ourselves. I'm Mick and my mate here, Harry, will clear a place in the back for you all."

They helped us into the van. Much to my embarrassment, as I negotiated the steps, my shoe caught on the door and the heel fell off. I gathered up the shoe and the offending heel as I stumbled unceremoniously into the back.

There we were standing among the boxes of chipped potatoes, fish, burgers, sausages, baps and minerals, and happy to be in from the cold. We swayed in motion with the van as it moved off. My sister and friends teased me by singing: 'You Picked a Fine Time to Leave Me Loose Heel.' I felt like a hen with distemper, standing with one leg higher than the other, but I brightened up and joined in as we all sang: 'We're Just A Travelling Indian Band.'

As we trundled along the snow-covered roads, the driver began laughing when he overheard me saying: "We're grateful for the lift, but it's a far cry from what I told that Strabane fellow I met."

I giggled as I went on: "I told him we'd travelled to the dance in Celine's Ford Capri."

"Why didn't you go the whole hog, Rosemary, and tell him that I drive a Mercedes?" she chipped in.

Arriving back in Burndennett, the boys helped us out of the van. "Well girls, it wasn't the comfort of a Ford Capri but it got you home," Mick said with a loud guffaw.

The next day, Mammy remarked several times on the very strong smell of fish and chips in the house. We didn't dare tell her that we'd been carted home in a chip van.

The following Saturday, as we were treating ourselves to minerals and chips in the Melody Inn café, in Strabane, I was gobsmacked when my Mr Brown Eyes walked in.

"Ah, fancy meeting you," he smiled. "Did your sister's Ford Capri not start in the snow then?"

"Why?" I stammered, my cheeks already red with embarrassment.

"My friend, Mick, the chip-van man, was telling me about giving four Burndennett girls a lift home and the laugh you all had about the Ford Capri," he said.

"I was chuffed that you think I have beautiful big brown eyes though," he winked at me as he walked on.

Rosemary McDermott is from Burndennet, near Strabane, Co Tyrone and is married with four sons. Her hobbies include writing and walking.

Butch Moore's Green Field Shock

Fred Molloy

D UBLIN in the very early 1960s was a hotbed of groups and showbands. The rules were simple – no alcohol inside dancehalls and if you looked dodgy, you didn't get past the bouncers.

My brother Mick was a drummer and I passed as a singer so we formed a little group with Paul Murphy on bass and Jack Lawlor on lead guitar. We got our first start playing as an interval band with the great Vic Mellows quartet who performed at most of the tennis club dances.

Within a short time I was approached by two representatives of a well-known band formally known as The Blue Clavons but were now called The Embassy 7.

The Clavons had put through their hands the likes of Dickie Rock and Butch Moore and now they wanted to try me out as lead vocalist with this re-formed band.

John Hardy, a brilliant musician and a great man, asked if I'd come to hear them play – they were the resident band for The Garda Boat Club at the Olympic Ballroom. Tom Ivory owned the venue and his claim to fame was he barred TJ Byrne and The Royal from ever playing there again. This followed a publicity stunt by TJ to get Brendan Bowyer into the papers. Seeing the fans go wild at his performance, he rang a number of journalists to tell them he was calling the Fire Brigade because the place was so over crowded that it was dangerous.

The press and the fire brigade arrived and met a very angry Tom Ivory. From that night he barred the Royal from playing at the Olympic, at a time when it was Dublin's best-known dance venue. I sang a few songs and apparently did alright. I was hired and started three weeks later.

*   *   *

John Hardy was a funny man and he got great mileage telling us about Butch's adventures when he was with the Clavons. They did a gig every week at the Teachers Club on Parnell Square, and come 11.15pm, John would nod for Butch to wind up as it was time for him to catch his last bus home. Such was the trappings of stardom back then.

John also told me of their first gig down the country. Butch sat silently looking out the window of the van. "John, why do cows and sheep graze in separate fields?" he asked innocently.

"Cows would eat the sheep if they were allowed into the same field together," John explained. Butch seemed to swallow the logic of this. However, on the way back an excited Butch roared: " John, look quick, there's cows and sheep together in the same field, stop the van."

The van didn't stop and neither did the laughter all the way back to Dublin.

We started a new band after some time called The Royalists but were advised to say we were from Ballyhaunis. It was from Mayo we started out, the hall packed to the ceiling. Our lead guitarist Kevin Vaughan was good and he loved that number Hoochie Coochie Man, probably because there was a lengthy guitar solo in it.

Kevin sang his song well, then he went into playing the guitar solo. He got a great reception except for five girls standing underneath us at the stage, who shouted: "Why don't ye play something like Larry Cunningham's Lovely Leitrim!"

To appease them a little later, I asked if they knew anyone they wanted to sing at the dance. They said Eddie O'Brien was great.

When I announced his name at the beginning of the next set, the place went bonkers. He sang Devil Woman and the crowd lapped him up. From then on in we were the greatest band in all of County Mayo.

The strangest gig we ever had to do came by way of a phone call to the Olympic where we were rehearsing one night after our day jobs.

I lifted the phone to hear a very excited Jimmy Flahive looking to speak to his brother, who wasn't rehearsing that night.

Jimmy was head of catering at Aer Lingus and later became famous with his cooking programme on RTÉ.

Flahive explained he'd organised a special day's golfing and dinner with dancing to follow but the quartet who were booked had let him down.

These were heavy-hitter types – managers and their wives from Ireland and America – and he begged for a replacement band. Hearing we were still in our work clothes, he promised to rustle up uniforms for us and provide washing and shaving facilities if we'd oblige him.

The five of us packed into Harry's smelly van and headed for the VIP lounge at Dublin Airport where on arrival we were stopped by suspicious security men who wouldn't allow us through until Jimmy arrived.

We did our ablutions quickly and then jumped into waiters' uniforms – they were all Jimmy could find.

We got through the first half of the show and as I made my way back to the stand during the interval, I was stopped by a lady who had enjoyed the free libations a little too much. "You know, you should think about becoming a singer instead of working as a waiter because you're not too bad," she said.

I told her I'd consider her advice and continued to hit the high notes for the rest of the night. I'm not sure if she felt I sounded better or worse, but I do know that Jimmy Flahive was one relieved man to be saved by a band he had cobbled together from a practice session.

Fred Molloy is a native Dubliner. Aside from music, he is an avid writer and has just completed his first novel.

Little Arrows

Bayveen O'Connell

SOME people say that the Beatles were responsible for awakening female hormones. Rubbish. I can tell you the exact moment I felt the full force of mine, a rosy spark ripped through me and there wasn't a Liverpudlian in sight. In the Arcadia on a sleety January night in 1962, out he came on stage and I just mauled this man with my eyes, my home-grown Warren Beatty: Brendan O'Brien of the Dixies.

As he swayed from side to side and strolled, microphone in hand, all the girls' faces would follow his every step. Then just as we were about to crack the windows, Joe Mac would jump forward all teeth and glasses and do the splits. Some theatrical diffusion, I'll say. In those days there was nowhere for a woman to scream, shriek, shout – not even a maternity ward. My God it felt great to give the old lungs a blast, to discover that my voice-box had an amplifier, dance 'til I couldn't feel my feet and pour out the doors with my ears ringing.

A South Presentation school girl with secretarial aspirations, I went in the doors in my mass scarf at eight o'clock and paid the 2/6 and left with my sweaty curls plastered to my face and a little too much cleavage on show from opening my blouse in the heat. A beast! A filthy Flintstone, I was, one step away from battling my way through a mob of girls four deep, towards the stage which I fully intended to climb up on to pounce on my love god.

When he got married I thought, well if I can't have Brendan to myself, I'd let Seán O'Donovan tame me. Didn't Sean grab my hand as the opening bars of 'Save the Last Dance' for me rang out? He was a gent, my Seán, even arranged for our wedding band to play 'Little Arrows' and my eyes just streamed as we danced. Later that night, much later, when we were more than half-sloshed and he had managed to help me out of my wedding dress without tearing any of the lace, we stood there giggling in our underwear. Out of nowhere came this black marker.

"Hold still," he said, and drew two arrows on the bare skin above my heart.

And I did the same on him only it was harder to see because he was a hairy bugger.

On our honeymoon weekend in Youghal, we sat looking out the hotel window as it lashed and our bathing suits hung dry and disembodied in the wardrobe. I didn't let Seán see me take the picture of the Dixies by the pool in Las Vegas from that morning's paper.

The day the news broke about the Miami Showband, I sat glued to the wireless nursing Brenda, while Sean Óg played at my feet. There was no dinner that evening when Seán came in and even though I had barely seen him crack an egg, he got out the pan and rustled up a fry for us. I heard him sniffling, turning the potato-bread. We snuggled and ate, all of us on the little couch in the kitchen, making a big comforting mess feeding one another. Nine months later another bundle arrived, and we thought it only right to call her Frances. On her first birthday, Seán played 'Clap your Hands and Stamp your Feet' so many times he broke the LP.

On our 35th anniversary down the local, I suggested getting the arrows as permanent tattoos and Seán nearly choked on his pint of Murphy's.

When he retired and the children had all settled in Canada, Oz and up the road, we would do the garden together. Seán clipped the hedges and I watered the flowerbed and the two of us would hum the lyrics 'I'm too old to work and too young to die.' All the songs we had in our heads, they haunted us but in the best way.

Bayveen O'Connell is a native of Sligo and loves music, writing and travelling. She has material published in The Sunday Independent, Ireland's Woman's Way and The Bohemyth literary journal.

Looking For The Shift

Maurice Crowley

I RISH dance halls were mostly purpose-built but in some cases they were converted mills or warehouses operated by a consortium of local business people who, in many cases, became very wealthy as a result.

One of the biggest operators in the business was Albert Reynolds, the former Taoiseach. Jim Hand and Jim Aiken owned halls such as Roseland in Moate, Horizon in Mullingar, and the Central in Tullamore. Dublin had the Tara Club, Irish Club and National Ballroom amongst others. The main objective of the night was to find a girlfriend, or for a girl to find a boyfriend, or to just get a snog or get 'shifted', as it was known. These venues were basic – you were there to dance!

There were rewards for those involved in the showband business. Most of the artists were signed up to Release Records. Managers attended gigs to collect the fee in notes on the night. There was no such thing as holidays, it was perform according to the diary bookings and this could find you travelling to Donegal tonight, Kerry tomorrow, Kildare next night, Dublin, Clare, Cork – just constantly on the go.

Many of the successful bands had the best of cars and would change them regularly due to high mileage. I recall one particular artist having a chauffeur-driven Jaguar. There were no contracts of employments in place, so if you were just an ordinary band member, you could be replaced without warning. If you took action against the management, you might never get a spot with another band as you'd be blacklisted. Rewards were good when times were good, but there were no reserves for the rainy day.

A good part of the lifestyle was the association and friendship that existed between bands. I recall meeting many of musicians during impromptu sessions after gigs. Bands met at different 'haunts' around the country. These were late houses/pubs/hotels where a band could knock any time and get a drink. This was wind down time for the lads and often ended up as an amazing session that could go on until six in the morning. Banter and crack and sometimes a singsong that would be simply amazing. I'd love to have some of the sessions recorded. Priceless stuff.

I recall a scary experience while travelling with a great friend of mine to a gig in Belfast. This was a few years after the Miami Showband massacre and bands had just begun to gig again in the North. I was driving his car that day as he had a broken leg so we travelled apart from the other lads. We left the midlands at 7am and were due to go directly to the recording studio in Belfast for 11am to put final touches to our next album. The gig that night in the Town Hall was at 9pm and we'd head for home around 2am.

It lashed out of the heavens all day. On the way home we came to a checkpoint on the border. My pal was fast asleep in the front seat. As I approached the barrier, I presumed an officer would just wave us on due to the brutal weather conditions. Two officers came out of the cabin and before we knew it, we were surrounded by at least three others. One approached my window and asked where I was going. He asked who was the person beside me and with that the passenger door was opened by one of the others. My buddy was ordered out of the car, and so was I. We were frisked, asked to remove our jackets and stand in the roadway in the torrential rain. We were soaked by then but they asked me to open the boot. The bass guitar was there with two band suits. They were taken out and thrown onto the road. They made us wait outside the vehicle for clearance as the officers returned to the cabin.

Half an hour later, they signalled for us to go. We gathered the ruined and soaked suits and guitar from the roadway, picked our jackets up and got into the car which was also soaked, as the doors were left open. It was scary, horrendous and totally brutal treatment but at least we were alive. Following the wetting that night, my buddy got pneumonia and was unable to work for a month.

Great names, great memories, great people, great music, great performances. It's good to see live Irish acts returning to the local stage and with the resurgence of talented Irish artists. I sometimes feel that although the big international artists give great performances, the value and intimacy is not there and not worth the massive fee imposed on the fans.

Great names such as Joe Dolan, Larry Cunningham, Roly Daniels, Ray Lynam, The Hillbillies, Dickie Rock, Butch Moore, Phil Begley, Glen Curtain, Paddy Cole, The Miami, The Indians, Brendan Shine, Big Tom, Swarbriggs, Two's Company, Cathal Dunne, Linda Martin, Margo, Susan McCann, The Capitol Showband, Red Hurley, and so many more, gave us such great memories. Recently, many of those great names have made a comeback and it is wonderful to see the support they get as they reprise great performances of yesteryear.

Let's hope it keeps going.

Maurice Crowley is from Dublin but has lived in Westmeath since 1970. He is a musician with great memories of the showband era. He dedicates this story to the memory of one particular musician, family man and close friend – Butch Moore.

52

A Hunger For
Love – And Food

Monica Fitzell

IN the late fifties the dancehall was the only place, well almost the only place, where boys and girls could meet. My tale is about how myself and three other late teen girls overcame difficulties in getting to our ballroom of romance.

In Kerry the social highlights were Puck Fair in South Kerry, Listowel Races and, the crème de la crème, the 15th of August, Pattern Day in Ballybunion. Getting to the local dancehalls was easy as we mostly cycled. However we really, really wanted to go to the Central Ballroom in Ballybunion on the 15th. The problem was transport, we lived in Lixnaw, and that was well outside bicycle range.

So we hatched a plot. We, each of us, would try and meet a lad at the local dancehall who had a car and would drive us to our destination on that big day. It worked. I met a boy who drove me home and an arrangement was made that we would meet again at the crossroads and hence on to Ballybunion. My friends and I dressed to the nines, hair bouffanted, dress with petticoats, heels and cardigan. However disaster was awaiting us. The boy never showed and an hour after the appointed time, we were devastated. We begged my father to give us a lift, but he said he had put in a hard day's work on the farm. He would rest by having a smoke of his pipe and a read of the Kerryman.

We walked to the main road again in the forlorn hope that someone, anyone, would stop and give us a lift to Ballybunion. As we approached a bend in the road, we came across a family of travellers sitting around a fire. Nothing remarkable about that ... until we saw they had a van. We approached in trepidation and asked if someone would drive us to our destination.

"Yes," the man said, he would do it for a consideration. We paid up, piled in and headed off through Listowel and on to Lisselton. Then he ran out of petrol. More money changed hands, we got fuel on board and on we sped to Ballybunion and our ballroom of dreams.

We had a great night of music and craic. There were people from Cork, Tipperary and a lot from Limerick. Amongst them was a fair sprinkling of not-so-young men.

They were the farmers who did not inherit land until late in life and were making a last ditch effort to find a wife. This was John B. Keane country. These men we avoided like the plague though we were duty bound to dance with whoever asked us.

Later that night we lodged with my Dublin aunties who had taken a house there for a fortnight's holiday. Next day I met my friend who was still in Ballybunion. We were all out of money and could only afford periwinkles to sustain us until we got a lift home to Lixnaw.

The hunger for love was now overtaken by the hunger for food.

Monica Fitzell is from Lixnaw, Co Kerry and is married with four grow- up children. Since retiring, she undertakes a little volunteer work in Citizens Information and St Vincent de Paul. She loves the great outdoors of her beloved Kingdom and often walks the beaches, woods and hills around her home area with her husband and extended family.

53

The Ghost Of
Dickie Rock

Ron Woods

' YOU don't have to be dead to haunt someone." My granny told me that when I was just a chiseller – or maybe I overheard her telling someone else – but I remember the phrase because she certainly said it often enough. She wasn't all that fond of unexpected visitors wandering into her house and when she'd eventually shooed them out with a 'Gaw bless love – you're welcome anytime' she'd close the door behind them and shuffle to her chair walking on the backs of her navy blue slippers muttering to herself: 'Gaw knows, you don't have to be dead to haunt someone – that woman never takes a hint to go.'

I suppose New Year's Eve is as good a time as any to reminisce. I can remember that and dozens of other moments from my childhood because of the sheer repetition, the endless routine nature of Irish life in the 1960s and early 70s. We'd had a longstanding agreement to meet up with a group of friends for the New Year. I'd said to herself :'If we don't organise something soon he's going to buy the tickets and we're going to end up spending New Year's Eve with Dickie bleeding Rock.'

We didn't, he did and now I'm here, standing outside in the smoking area of the Regency Hotel counting down the last few hours of 2015. Still, I suppose it's better than sitting at home watching the pre-recorded merriment of beautiful people having a better time than we ever could on Jools Holland's Hootenanny... again. At least this is real.

Of course, I never had any interest in Dickie Rock or any other Irish band when I was growing up. None of it was worth listening to as far as I was concerned, but it was impossible to avoid.

Dickie seemed to be everywhere then and this is my point about being haunted. He was huge; Eurovision, The Late Late. Every time you turned on Radio Éireann if it wasn't Gloria singing One Bleedin' Day at a Time then it was him.

My only chance to escape was Radio Luxembourg. Even when you found it the signal crackled and faded in and out, but by ever so gently twisting the knob you could follow the music until it fizzled out completely and then return the dial to its original position and wait for it to come back. Crackle crackle... 208 Once an hour Power Play... crackle crackle.

It was 1972 before I discovered real music as opposed to pop and by that I mean my first time sitting down and listening to an entire album, David Bowie's Hunky Dory, over and over again. And when I say listen, I mean listen. Leaning forward, watching the shining vinyl revolve under the stylus, Bowie's other-worldly face on the label doing 360s, leaning in so close that you could smell the heat of the turntable motor. It was a little trip in itself, it felt like your head would disappear into the music instead of the other way round. What an album to be your first, and what a decade for music. I was into everything from prog rock to heavy metal and back again. Rick Wakeman to Black Sabbath, Deep Purple to The Strawbs.

I take another drag on my cigar. I got a present of a pack of small Cuban cigars for Christmas so I thought it might be nice to bring them along and share a couple to celebrate the night that's in it, but himself being an actual genuine reformed smoker and all he won't touch them, so I'm on me own. I've no intentions of spending too long out here but you've no idea how slowly a good cigar burns. It just isn't possible to smoke one fast. And anyway, a smoking area is not the worst place in the world to spend your evening, eavesdropping on other people's lives. I've got myself into a snug corner just behind the door where I can set my pint on a low wall beside me and stand out of the way. It's a breezy chilly night and this is about the most sheltered spot to be had. The comings and goings of the other smokers is keeping me entertained.

"Can I have a light, love?"

A tiny woman with the wrinkled skin of a 90-year-old but who might only be 70 has manoeuvred herself in front of me. She has one of those tripod walking sticks that looks slightly comical when she leaves it standing on its own. I light her cigarette. She takes three little puffs and closes her eyes. Then another three puffs followed by a watery bubbling cough. She opens her eyes and catches me looking at her.

"I'm cuttin' back," she says. "Emphysema."

"I don't usually smoke at all," I say, lifting my cigar to her. "Special occasions only."

"I'm on oxygen at home you know," she says, seeming proud of that particular fact. "Me son says that if I keep smokin' with the tank switched on I might go out with a bang." Another bubbly cough. "God love him, he's an awful worrier."

Two blonde women done up to the nines burst out through the door in fits of laughter about something one of them has just said or done. A draft of warm air and music follows them out. They've only just lit up when the door swings open again and they're joined by a grey-haired man in his shirtsleeves, the 30 inch belt of his trousers pulled up tight under a 36 inch waist. He's a lot more interested in them than they are in him and he positions himself in their little group so he can keep an eye on the door. Whenever it opens his eyes flick guiltily toward it. The women remind me of my aunties.

When I was a kid every adult friend of my parents was referred to as Auntie or Uncle. I must have been into my early teens before I realised just how small our extended family really was. Every so often two or three of these aunties would arrive in together and take over our entire house to get ready for some big night out. Tables, shelves, mantelpiece, the arms of the couch, even the top of the telly would be covered in bottles of all sizes, tubes and tubs, brushes and combs. They'd stand in front of the mirror over the fireplace taking it in turns to create elaborate beehive hairdos for each other. Steel combs with vicious looking pointed ends were flicked and twirled between fingers as layers upon layers of hair were carefully built up and held in place with unlimited quantities of hair lacquer. I think they bought the lacquer in bulk and then transferred it into small plastic bottles -you had to squeeze the actual bottle to generate a spray mist – it was highly flammable and almost certainly toxic for a child. The final result sat so high on their heads that it might be an exaggeration to say their hair touched the ceiling but they definitely had to duck to get out the door.

They would have been going to The Top Hat in Dún Laoghaire, it was near to where we lived. All of their talk seemed to be about shows they'd already been to or were planning to go to. The Royal, or was it The Miami, or maybe The Miami were playing in The Royal? None of it really made any sense to me and I didn't care. I was just mesmerised by their technicolour glamour in my black and white world.

Later, much later, the one real Auntie tottered on high-heels up to the stage at my wedding to sing one of Dickie's big hits, 'The Candy Store.' It has a simple romantic lyric that someone set down to a depressing, funereal melody. Every time I hear it I expect at least one of the young lovers to die tragically and only make it to the 'Chapel on the Hill' in a coffin.

"Are you a fan of Dickie?" My new best friend is looking up at me and I notice now that she has huge brown eyes. They remind me of one of my other aunties that wasn't.

"Eh, not really," I say it quietly, it seems a bit rude to say it out loud.

A little earlier the band had been playing a few warm-up songs when we arrived so I'd taken the opportunity to nip up a flight of stairs to the gents. Of course I was cutting it fine timewise and as I'm heading out, the band leader is making a big to-do about introducing the main man. All 6'1" of me is charging up the stairs looking at me feet when I meet Dickie coming down, all smiles, looking out toward the stage. I came within half an inch of trampling him into the carpet. That would have made a good headline: 'Dickie crushed by man who says he's not really a fan.'

"I'm the same age as him," she says, "same birthday too, well same day different month."

"Getaway. He must be 90," I say. "You look a lot younger."

"Feck off!"

Dickie hasn't stopped singing since he got on stage. Every time the door opens I hear a different song. I couldn't name a single one of them for you now and yet I know them all. There's a familiarity about them. It's like there was never a time I didn't know them.

There's quite a few smokers coming and going, all locals by the sound of them, so the English accent, when I hear it, stands out. As we all know, Article 29 of Bunreacht na hÉireann states, inter alia, that Irish Nationals must at all times be polite and welcoming to visitors, especially English visitors to whom we must be over-polite, inviting them into the front room and avoiding, where possible, any mention of 800 years of blah blah blah.

The woman has an unmistakable Yorkshire accent and when someone fulfils their national civic duty by asking her where she's from she replies "Redcar."

I know Redcar well for its racecourse but I can't help myself. "Where's that?"

"Just outside Middlesbrough," she explains.

I shake my head.

"Hartlepool?" she tries again.

I purse my lips and look confused. There's nothing in the constitution that says we can't take the piss.

"Sunderland? You must know Sunderland."

She's obviously working her way, city by city, up the east coast of England. "Oh Right Sunderland, yeah," I say. "That's in Wales, isn't it?"

This is too easy. She gives me a look but seems happy enough to be the centre of attention. She tells us all that herself and her husband are over here on a New Year's Eve special. Bed and breakfast and entertainment to ring in the New Year. She takes another long drag on her cigarette, then points her finger at the door behind me and in a staccato of exhaling smoke and words she asks: "Who's that chap singing on stage?"

It takes me a moment to understand the question. It's as if she's just asked why it gets dark at night. Does she really not know?

Everyone else turns to look at me, wondering what I'm going to say.

"Dickie Rock," I say. "That's Dickie Rock."

She looks at me like I should have more to say.

"Do you not know him?" I ask. She shakes her head.

"He's like your Tom Jones only more famous," I add. I'm thinking; how does she not know Dickie Rock, our Dickie Rock, my Dickie Rock? After all, isn't he a national treasure from our showband days?

Ron Woods is a Dublin short story writer. He has been twice short-listed for the Hennessy New Irish Writing Awards and selected for The Lonely Voice in the Irish Writers' Centre.

The Magic Of The Banba

Catherine Murphy

MY father, Thomas Traynor, was born in Shercock, Cavan in 1918 and my mother, Catherine Foley, in Caragh Lake, Kerry in 1924. Both were sociable but Mum was also a private person, seldom giving away much about her youth.

Dad was happy to share anecdotes and gave various accounts of how he met Mum – we weren't sure what to believe.

In 1993, he was nominated as a contributor to an exhibition at The Grange Museum, Neasden, London on the theme of emigration to Britain. He told the curator the authentic version of meeting Mum. He also talked about people working hard and socialising in dancehalls. He mentioned The Banba, Kilburn, (now Sainsbury's), run by Mayo men. He said a Sligo man, Johnny Muldoon, had several dancehalls, including The Shannon, Belsize Road and another in Hammersmith. His club on Tottenham Court Road had a basement and acted as an air-raid shelter so he could keep it open throughout the war.

There were also four-penny dances in Quex Road hall (attached to The Church of the Sacred Heart, Kilburn) with star turn, Pat Keogh's Céilí Band. A Cavan man had The Emerald and The Pride of Erin close to Hammersmith Palais. Then there was Paddy Casey from Sneem, Kerry, one of seven famous Crusher Casey brothers, heavyweight wrestling champions; proprietor of: The Glocamora, Bayswater, The Inisfree, Ealing Broadway, The Shamrock Club in Elephant and Castle.

There was a dancehall known as Burtons above the tailor shop on Cricklewood Lane, which Mick O'Dea from Castleisland, Kerry owned, subsequently taken over by Mossie Byrne becoming The Galtymore.

Famous showman, Butty Sugrue, converted Kilburn's Grange Cinema to 'Butty's Club and Dance Hall' before the re-branding by Tipperary's Carey Brothers as The National.

My father, then a builder and decorator, had lived in London for years and had a wealth of knowledge of the social scene. He'd just completed a job with a Cork friend, who went to draw their money. They arranged to meet outside The Princess of Wales (now The Lillie Langtry) on the corner of Belsize Road and Abbey Road, Kilburn.

Taking up the story of how he met his wife-to-be whilst waiting, I'll continue in Dad's own words. "She was coming along with another girl who'd seen me at The Banba a few times. Kathleen piped up: 'We'll be there tonight – at The Banba.'

"Well, I never danced. I hadn't a step and I wouldn't go into the dancehalls until I had a few drinks in me, you see, but I went to meet her. It was her first day over from Ireland."

My aunt claimed that people said my mother was "the prettiest girl ever to come out of Killorglin."

Mum told me she loved dancing in Kerry. She'd left home to work in Tralee and cycled to dances. The country lanes were a far cry from her destination in London, whereas by this time, Dad knew every inch of the metropolis. On arrival, Mum told him she'd heard of the famous 'Banba' and was intent on going there.

I think it's fun and ironic that although she'd just come to town she was always a strong woman and knew from the outset what she wanted. Dad was genial and prepared to overcome the dread of dancing to get the girl. It was romantic they met on her first day in London – fate!

They married in 1948 and were great parents to my brother, Brian, my sister, Ann, and I. When they were courting, Cavan beat Kerry in the famous 1947 All Ireland in New York's Polo Grounds, with Dad's relation by marriage, Peter Donohoe, named Man of the Match. Mum and Dad didn't fall out over county rivalry... she had zero interest in sport as she was so busy dancing.

Tommy and Kathleen became proactive members of the Irish community, working for decades in the local Catholic school and contributing to establishing The Marian Community Centre in 1975. My sister and I put in shifts behind the bar; keeping us company on the other side of the counter were our future husbands, Gerry Stack and Kevin Murphy while the Siege of Ennis or jiving went on around them.

Mum had five sisters and four brothers. History repeated itself when her youngest sister, the very attractive Bridget Foley came to London, aged 15. When she was employed at Wall's sausage factory, Acton, west

London in the 1950s, she caught the eye of workmate Jimmy 'Plum' Flynn. He showed great determination in pursuing her but she was having none of it for a long time and then had a change of heart.

The magic of The Banba struck again. Bridget was at the dancehall one Sunday afternoon. Jimmy was there, too, fashionably dressed as a Teddy Boy. This gave Bridget the idea he'd be a great dancer. Always witty, he came over with the dubious invitation: "Do you want your feet trampled on?"

According to Bridget: 'He couldn't cross one leg over the other and he did trample on my feet.' After that Jimmy left the dancing to Bridget. "I went to the dances and could dance with anyone I liked; he went to the pub and we met up later," she explained.

It obviously worked for them since they married in 1960 and went on to be parents to my lovely cousins; Karen, James, twins – Emma and Paul – and Betty. They've also got good dance moves – it must be in the genes from their mother.

The Flynn clan is here thanks to their parents' romance. Again fate had a hand. Bridget reveals of The Banba: "It was the first and last time I was there – we preferred The Galtymore."

Catherine Murphy (née Traynor) was born in Kilburn, London when it was affectionately known as the '33rd county of Ireland'. Married to Kevin, she is a retired Communications Manager but volunteers representing Irish Spectrum Radio, a London-based station, with outreach to the Irish diaspora worldwide.

55

Future Taoiseach Comes To Our Rescue

Neil Owens

O N New Year's Night 1963, my brother Liam, my cousin, John Joe Kearns, and I decided to travel from our home in Lismehy at the foothills of Sliabh Bawn, near Strokestown, to see the Capitol Showband performing the Roseland Ballroom in Moate, Co. Westmeath.

Liam, who worked in Dublin, was an avid fan and knew all the band members as he had met them at various venues in the city. It was his idea to go to Moate. I was the proud owner of a 1948 Ford Anglia – that black high box-type saloon car with the head lamps perched on the two large wings and the single red rear light positioned in the centre of the boot lid.

It was my first car and it was with some trepidation we set off on this perilous journey on a dark frosty night.

The dance was enjoyable and there were lots of women looking for romance. However, none of our encounters blossomed into anything of a lasting nature. When the dance was over, we set off for home. A short distance outside Moate, we hit a patch of black ice and the car went into an uncontrollable skid, turning 180 degrees and ending up sideways in a deep drain. John Joe shouted: "We're for it now – we'll all be killed!"

My brother Liam, who was in the back, seemed to find the whole incident hilarious and started giggling, whereupon John Joe shouted: "It's no laughing matter!" As the car was a two-door, we had to climb out by opening the passenger door upwards which reminded us a bit like a pilot exiting the cockpit of small aircraft. A few passers-by stopped to help us in trying to get the vehicle back on the road, but our efforts were fruitless.

We walked back to the Roseland and got talking to Albert Reynolds. He and his brother Jim had a number of dancehalls in the midlands at the time. Albert agreed to give us a lift and to his eternal credit dropped us off at our door in the early hours of the morning.

In the days following, we engaged a garage in Moate to retrieve the car and replace a track rod end which had come out the worse for wear in the episode.

I moved to Canada in the mid-sixties and during the 1994 World Cup in the US, a group of us were in attendance at the Italian game in the Meadow Lands in New Jersey. After the game we were walking through a Casino which is part of the sports complex when we happened upon Albert, who was Taoiseach by then, with his press secretary, Seán Duignan and security personnel. As there were few people around at this stage after the game, he stopped to talk to our group and take pictures. He had gone a long way out of his way to give us a lift home from Moate to Lismehy way back in 1963 but now finally I was about to get the chance to thank him.

Neil Owens comes from Lismehy, Strokestown, Co Roscommon but now lives in Schomburg, Ontario, Canada. A retired carpenter, he likes travelling and reading and visits Ireland regularly.

56

The Art Of Free Admission To Dances

Peter Gordon

WORKING in Mohill in the 1950s and 1960s was not very profitable. However the education provided was the equivalent of third level while the entertainment was nothing short of hilarious due to the amazing characters that frequented the shop.

The low pay saw many people devise ingenious systems to get free admission to places of entertainment. These 'systems' included getting in windows or walking in backways so that the doorman thought the person was going out. That never worked!

Another trick was to walk in carrying a musical instrument pretending to be a member of the band. That did!

*　　*　　*

Canon MJ Masterson, the Parish Priest of Mohill in the 1940s and 1950s was a very saintly man. He never asked the parishioners for a donation which meant that when he died, there was no money in the parish funds. The Church, the Canon's house, the curate's house and the parish hall were all in a state of semi-dereliction.

The Bishop became aware of the situation and appointed Canon Wall to the parish. Amongst his terms of reference was the restoration of parish properties. On his first Sunday he revealed that the Bishop was alarmed at the work required to renovate them. Parishioners were asked to contribute which was a bit of a culture shock to them. One of the curates, Fr. Gill, was delegated to raise funds by running dances in the parish hall. He booked bands but most of them were hopeless and Fr. Gill, as an excellent musician himself, knew this only too well. When people complained to him that the bands were hopeless he would reply haughtily: "The only music they ever heard were mugs falling off the dressers, sure they wouldn't know the Tantum Ergo from The Boys of Wexford!"

Running dances on a Sunday night was not a good idea as the Cloudland Ballroom in Rooskey and the Mayflower Ballroom in Drumshanbo also held dances on that night. The big difference was these venues had Ireland's top showbands as attractions. Parishioners felt obliged to support the local dance, although doing so was often tortuous.

During one such outing, four lads asked me if I would drive them to the Mayflower, where the Johnny Quigley All Stars from Derry were playing. I agreed on one condition – that they had to use their initiative to get in for free.

They were all up for it and piled into my trusty red Volkswagen Beetle. On arriving in the car park at the Mayflower, the local Sergeant, Michael Waters came over to greet me. We were both on the county hurling board. At the time, our GAA club, of which I was secretary, was having a "difference of opinion" with the football board.

As a mark of protest we were supporting Sgt. Waters for the chairmanship of the football board and he thanked me for that. In return, I asked him to walk in with me to the ballroom. He was a very tall man and I think the doorman didn't see me walking beside him.

Johnny Quigley was reputed to be the best clarinet player in Ireland at that time. He grew a beard and was nicknamed the 'Londonderry Hair.' Johnny played solos to which the great Hall Moffat also danced solo. Hall's dancing, which he created himself, was a mixture of Sean-Nos, Jitterbug and the Charleston. More people were looking at Hall than were dancing. When Johnny finished playing a number, it was Hall that got the applause and rightly so.

The stewards wanted to stop Hall from doing his solo dancing but he said that he'd paid his admission fee in but as the girls wouldn't dance with him, he elected to dance solo.

After a while I went up to the restaurant for a tea and sandwich. Who should I see at one of the tables having their supper with one of the ballroom directors, only two of the lads I brought – Johnny Rowley and Seán Sheridan. Both were progressive farmers and were cattle experts.

The ballroom director was a part-time farmer and had advertised a few cattle for sale in the 'Leitrim Observer' that week. Johnny posed as a cattle dealer named Willie Leonard from Castlederg, County Tyrone. On arriving at the ballroom he asked for the advertiser of the cattle who arrived in a few minutes. They discussed the details of the cattle and made an appointment to meet the next day to complete the deal. Johnny pretended to walk away, then turned to enquire if there was any where they could get a cup of tea. At that, our heroes were brought in – admission free of course – and got their supper into the bargain. If my memory serves me right, they got the other two in, saying they were helpers.

So the four had been true to their word by getting in free just like me.

* * *

The next day I met Johnny as he was cycling up the Main Street of Mohill. "You better hurry or you will be late for your appointment outside Drumshambo," I shouted

He waved as he peddled on.

Who needed money for admission when you could come up with stories like that?

Peter Gordon is a retired business man and father of five grown-up children. A proud Leitrim man living in Dublin, his hobbies include gardening, walking the dog and supporting Leitrim GAA teams.

Crash, Bang, Wallop
At 'The Arc'

Bunty Flynn

IT was Christmas week in the early sixties, my friend Kay who was two years older than I was, called on her way home from work.

"How would you like to hear a real Showband?" she asked with her eyes bulging with excitement? "The Dixies are in the Arcadia on St. Stephen's night. My brother is taking the car and my mother will let me go if you will come with me so as I won't be the only girl with the lads."

"You've got to be joking, my father won't let me go to a dance," I said.

My father was a fiddle player and held Irish music sessions regularly in our house. He had an aversion to jazz and modern music and his friend Mick who played the uileann pipes said the music was only "fit for shoneens." When I tuned the radio to Radio Luxembourg he flew into a rage that such an uncultured sound would enter the kitchen.

"Don't touch that wireless again. I don't want that jungle music in this house," he warned. Then he'd turn the dial of the brown Bakelite to Radio Éireann and listen to Seán Maguire playing 'The Blackbird' or the 'Mason's Apron,' his foot tip-tapping to the music.

Kay lowered her voice to a whisper: "Pretend that you are staying with me for the night to keep my mother company, Christmas can be so lonely for some people, you know." Her mother had been widowed two years previously and this was a plausible enough excuse to stay overnight.

Permission was given for the overnight stay and so the packing began. I carefully folded my red cotton dress with the white polka dots and its white bolero jacket with the starched underskirt and placed them in a paper bag and hid them under my nightdress, wool jumper and sensible shoes for my stay. The blue eyeshadow, black mascara and red lipstick was stuffed into my slippers with the panstick tan makeup. With instructions to go to bed early and help Kay's mother with the dishes, my

CRASH, BANG, WALLOP AT 'THE ARC'

mother waved me off on my bike that Stephen's Day, my precious cargo tied carefully on the carrier.

Kay, being older, supervised my make-up when I arrived at her house and also loaned me her white strappy sandals with the peep-toes. These added an extra two inches to my height. I felt a million dollars as I twirled around the bedroom. A final check up in the hall mirror revealed a very tanned, grown up me with panda eyes under a row of kiss curls that were set so rigidly in place they could outdo Bill Haley. Then we piled into the old Hillman car, Kay's brother Pat at the wheel and drove off. His three friends, cigarettes dangling James Dean-like from pale faces, were already packed in the back.

It may have been a frosty night outside but the atmosphere was red-hot in the Arc as The Dixies began playing. The dancers, like wriggling sardines, jived and sent a jet of steam soaring towards the large glitterball hanging from the vast ceiling.

Joe McCarthy (Joe Mac) brought the house down with his comedic 'Santa! Where's Me Bike?' rendition, followed by 'The Banks of My Own Lovely Lee' which had the crowd swaying and singing along as if they were at an All-Ireland final. There was almost a stampede towards the girls when they struck up 'Love Me Tender.' Girls doing strong lines draped their arms over their boys' necks and laid their cheeks on their shoulders as they danced. The half-serious ones placed two flat hands on the chest of their partners and the 'Don't be getting any notions ones' held their arms fully extended on the boys' shoulders.

Then the tempo changed once more and the crowd jived to 'Rock Around the Clock' and 'Blue Suede Shoes.' Finally, at 2am came the last dance and with a "Goodnight, God Bless, safe home and happy dancing from the Dixies"... the night of magic was over.

Reluctantly, we got into the car and started singing and swaying to the radio music as we made our way towards home. Then in a split second everything changed. Without warning, gravel and stones crunched and spat as the car turned and spun and landed on its side in a ditch. As I tried to focus I could see one of my "strappy sandals" hanging like a bauble on the gear stick on the steering column. Through the enormous gap of what remained of the windshield, I looked out to see frost coated trees standing sentry all around us.

Ironically, as we surveyed the crash, the car radio played Fats Domino singing 'I want to walk you home.'

I wished.

In the haze, another car stopped beside us and a voice shouted: "Turn off the bloody engine or she'll go up."

A short time later came the sound of an ambulance. "Hang on," a confident voice shouted. "You will be fine, we will have you out in no time."

Like all good and even bad liars, my thoughts immediately turned to self-preservation. Inevitably, I forgot all arguments as to whether God was a He or a She as I implored Him to save me from the wrath of my father.

We were taken to Fermoy Hospital and admitted to a ward. The doctor told us we would have to stay overnight for observation. When I woke up the following morning my father and mother were standing at the end of the crisp white bed, my mother crying silently as my father played with his hat across his fingertips.

Seeing me move, he blurted out: "I'm glad you're alright, but that damn foreign music is the cause of all of this."

"Will you shush, Pat," my mother intoned. "Didn't you see the state of the car as we passed it – they are lucky to be alive. Oh my God, will you look at her two black eyes."

I did not want to enlighten her just then, that some of that black was mascara. And so very subdued, with a sprained ankle and two very swollen eyes, I entered the taxi that my car-less father had to hire, to get us home.

The valley at the foot of the Galtee Mountains never looked so inviting as that morning but I was suffused with a sense of great sorrow that we had crashed and I had been found out in a lie by my parents.

I wasn't sorry though that I had been to 'The Arc' and heard the Dixies. As we continued our journey towards Mitchelstown, there was part of me already looking forward to hearing The Dixies again... but first we'd let the dust settle.

Bunty Flynn is a retired playschool teacher and lives in Mitchesltown, Co Cork where she is married with three children and four grandchildren. Her hobbies include writing short stories and playing golf.

Stiletto Heels And The Melody Aces

Betty Devenney

I ALWAYS enjoyed seeing the older girls from my street leaving for the dance each weekend. Wearing stiletto heeled shoes and all dolled-up, they were full of glamour.

A favourite band back then was The Melody Aces. I was proud because my daddy played the tenor saxophone and clarinet for them. My hope was there would be bands and stiletto heels still around when I was old enough to go dancing.

Sometimes the band travelled to England to play the dancehalls there. Then, you watched for the postman every day to bring the promised postcard from Daddy.

Many years have passed now and I still have his diaries. Browsing through them made me realise how much travelling they did across the Irish Sea. One date I noticed was for January 4, 1959 at The Galtymore in Cricklewood. They were back again in March 1961, and November of the same year and played there quite a few times the following year. The last diary entry is for 1963.

There was an abundance of popular dancehalls all around the country, and before my own dancehall days, I would hear the girls calling out to each other: "Where are you for tonight and who's playing?"

The Orchid in Lifford or the Butt Hall in Ballybofey might feature while Borderland was another favourite, even though the only way to get there sometimes was to thumb a lift.

The Melody Aces played many times at The Rainbow Ballroom in Glenfarne, Co Leitrim, the original 'Ballroom of Romance.' The Palladrome in Strabane had a great floor for dancing on. Crowds came from across the border and Derry to dance there... and many met the love of their life at this popular place.

I still remember the click of stiletto heels on the pavement as the older girls set out to dance the night away there. The layers of petticoats they wore underneath their dresses bounced and swished with every step they took. It was a sight worth seeing with their hair backcombed to within an inch of its life. If long enough it could be constructed into a beehive or smoothed into a bouncy sleek style, curled at the ends or flicked out.

Essential items in every handbag was a Max Factor powder compact, a mirror, much needed when powdering the nose or applying the very important lipstick for that first love kiss. Another essential was the hair lacquer, which kept a hairstyle in place. More preferable was a hair spray, but that was too expensive to buy. I found all this out later, along with dancing around my handbag, to keep it safe, when my own dance hall adventures came around.

When the time eventually came to go dancing, it was the mid-sixties and Mary Quant was the new fashion guru. The style of dress and shoes had changed, and I stepped out in my longed-for stiletto heels. The Beatles and Roy Orbison were blaring from the wireless. Record shops were buzzing with teenagers listening to the hits of the day.

The band performing at my first grown up dance at the Palindrome was The Cadets. Their outfits were amazing, and Eileen Reid's blonde hair was swept up into the highest beehive I'd ever seen.

Back then the heat from the crowds became so intense, that dancing really was cheek to cheek. If a boy asked if he could buy you a mineral, and you liked him and said yes, you had a date for the night. Depending on how things went, it was a date that lasted for the rest of your life.

In the ladies-room the atmosphere was always electric, with girls checking their make-up, discussing the talent and hoping some special fella would ask them for a date. The scent of 'Tweed' or 'Panache' or maybe 'Soir De Paris' mingling intoxicatingly in the air, gave a flavour to the excitement and anticipation of those moments.

'Pagan' was a popular perfume at the time and some girls claimed the scent alone could capture the heart-throb you had your eye on.

It never worked for me.

Sometimes a photographer would be go around the dance floor asking couples if they would like to have their snaps taken. My boyfriend and I had our photo taken at a dance in the Palladrome. The year was 1965 and we were just 17 though in our own minds, we thought we were all grown up.

I smile now when I look at that photo because we are still together, forever 17 inside our heads, and forever dancing 52 years later.

Sometimes we even imagine the music is being played by Daddy and the Melody Aces – and I'm still wearing my stiletto heeled shoes.

Betty Devenney is from Strabane Co Tyrone. Married to Danny she has four children. Her hobbies are painting, gardening and creative writing. She's a member of the Gateway Writers Group, Lifford.

Some Dance To Remember, I Danced To Forget

Joan Griffin

UNLIKE most people, I saw the opportunity to go to a dance as an escape from home, not as a place where I deliberately set out to meet someone. However the fact that I did meet someone very special was a bonus for me but it wasn't without complications.

I emigrated to England in 1952 and got a living-in job in Middlesex. I was married at the time to my first husband and we came home for Christmas.

When it was time to head for the boat again he told me: "I'm not going back." I made it clear to him that with or without him, I was returning but I had to leave my two little girls at home with my mother.

Shortly after I returned I began to feel sick so I knew then that child No. 3 was on the way. That time it was hard to get reasonable accommodation as the landlady, who was from Scotland, didn't want me there when she heard I was pregnant again. She gave me until the end of the week to get out.

Eventually I went to a place which was owned by a Greek man who treated us very well. When we moved from there, we got a prefab from the Council that had all the amenities. Johnny, my husband, was back in England and, I think, was up in Yorkshire. Like many Irish, he was fond of the drink and soon returned to London.

By this time, I had the girls back in England with me. I told them they could have the double room with double bed and the bunk bed. They were delighted. I told my husband he could have a room for himself and stressed that the other room was mine. I warned him not to put his nose near my door again or I'd hit him over the head. We were finished as a couple. We would move onwards and hopefully upwards but not as husband and wife anymore.

It was tough and lonesome trying to work and rear kids but I did it because I had no alternative. Then after many years when the girls had gotten bigger, I decided that I owed it to myself to get out now and then for a break. I chose a Wednesday night in the early sixties to go up to St Olive's Hall in Manor House.

By then, I had my driver's licence and had a mini car of my own. In the dance, I met a guy from Kerry. We danced and he propositioned me for a bed and breakfast up the road. "Aye," I said, "and what else?"

Later that evening when the dance was over, I met another Kerryman called Sonny who told me he would walk me over to the bus stop. But I crossed the road and told him I had my own car. "Where I come from they don't even have their own bikes," he laughed.

He was living in digs with a fella from Mayo. He asked me if I went out much to the dances and I told him I'd meet him the following week in St Olive's.

We did that and then I arranged to go to the pub for a lemonade on another night.

Sonny had just lost his mother and we talked for hours about our various situations. He was a great listener and encouraged me to get out and enjoy myself. Over time, we ended up doing a tour of the halls; the Galtymore, the Gresham, the Loyola, the Blarney. I couldn't truthfully tell you who played in any of those venues when we went. All I know is it got me out of the house and it helped me forget everything for a few hours.

Now there was nothing whirlwind about the way our courtship took off; it became a thing for me to meet up with him in this manner over a 10-year period between 1963 and 1973.

At that stage we had obviously become pretty close and I decided that I would get a divorce. We followed that up by getting married on May 8, 1973 in Highbury Town Hall.

We also decided that we'd like to return to Ireland and it took a while but we finally got back to Waterford to live in 2001.

It was great for me to settle back into the parish of Kilmeadan and Sonny also loved being back in Ireland.

We got on very well with the people and the parish priest even told me he wanted to ordain me a Eucharistic minister. I agreed to do visitations to the old people, but I told him I would not give out communion from the altar.

I always knew Sonny was a gentleman and that really shone through when my first husband died. There was the expense of getting him home from England. For a while it was all up in the air about who would pay until Sonny said we would look after the cost of shipping him home and paying for his burial here.

Johnny, God rest him, knew my mother long before he had ever met me and his wish was to be buried in her plot in Ballyduff Lower.

Some people might find this hard to believe but behind it all, we were friends in life and why wouldn't we be friends in death as well? Sonny and I were delighted to be able to do that much for him.

Sometime later we decided that we now could have a church wedding to go with the civil one we had in England in 1993. Sonny joked that after being with me for so long, he wanted to make an honest woman of me. That wedding took place in 2003 and we had the reception in the school that I attended as a child. The Memphis band provided the music for us on that illustrious occasion and everyone had a ball.

We also held a reception for our many English and Welsh friends in Fishguard. We had been driving in and out of the port for over 40 years and it was lovely to meet the people who honoured us with their presence at our function.

Joan Griffin, nee Aulsberry, is a native of Ballyduff, Kilmeadan, Co Waterford and lived for over 50 years in London. On June 1, she celebrated her 86th birthday. A mother of three girls, her hobbies include reading and dancing and she loves to listen to country music She has an extensive record collection stretching to several hundred pristine albums.

A Diabolical Intervention
Or Divine Inspiration?

Joe Keane

THE 1950s was a decade dominated by crozier power, De Valera and censorship. The Lenten season required the faithful to abstain from dancing during this dismal spell of over-zealous piety.

Those of us who were domiciled in foreign parts, however, enjoyed greater freedom of social expression. It helped in a small way to overcome the home sickness. Some of us danced to the likes of Ken McIntosh in the old Mecca Ballroom in Leicester Square. Kenny Ball was also very popular. But despite the romantic setting of such post-war entertainment, there was something lacking as the dancers seemed isolated from the formal stage setting.

That was about to change with the arrival of the showband era. The new sound was progressive and vibrant, and before long engulfed the entire island. In due course, the Galtymore in Cricklewood and the Banba in Kilburn resonated to the strains of the Royal and the Drifters. Doc Carroll and the Royal Blues were particular favourites with West of Ireland patrons.

The Casino Ballroom in Castlerea drew fans like a magnet. The owner Joe McLoughlin was possessed of great entrepreneurial spirit, long before it became the much bandied expression of today. Cutting a dapper figure in a smart suit, he was firm but fair in his transactions. He had one very strict regulation regarding passes. Those could not be handed over to third parties as was often the case in other venues.

In the sixties, we were besieged with a series of violent storms. One Sunday night in particular remains indelibly imprinted in my mind. In my battered old Ford, we set sail for The Casino. A storm had knocked power lines and fallen trees were strewn on the roads. Miraculously we arrived unscathed but to our dismay, the place was in darkness. Soon though an innovative management had put in place a remedial plan. The double doors were opened wide so that smaller cars could be positioned to provide essential illumination inside. This continued until the dance was over with a relay of cars responding to the lighting emergency. A first in terms of creative genius for sure.

Walshe's Ballroom in Charlestown was another popular venues for our contemporaries. One of our companions, albeit reluctantly, was an older chap called Danny. He was a tee-totaller and had something of a humour by-pass.

This appealed to our mischievous nature and often resulted in some outrageous pranks at his expense. This ballroom had banned the playing of requests, as it often resulted in bad blood between rival parties. We found a way around this regulation. One night we sent a note up on the stage informing the attendance of a forthcoming dance in a local hall. The band was only too happy to oblige.

The trouble was the fictitious other band was called after Danny's surname and the venue was in fact his townland. The spectacle of Danny's face on hearing the request while out dancing still evokes a hilarious memory. He must have jumped two feet off the floor in rage.

On one occasion our sense of practical joking backfired. We attended a carnival in Ballymote in Sligo where a pub exemption was in place. Unfortunately we partook a little too liberally of the available alcohol. By the time we arrived at the marquee, the dance was over. Then who should we see outside, but Danny. We asked him, quite genuinely, if we could offer him a lift home. Out of a sense of desperation, he accepted.

Although we were foolish in many ways, we were always careful to park in a safe place. On this night we picked the most secure place of all – the parish priest's driveway. However, with the drink on board, none of us could remember where we had parked. Vainly we tried place after place, careful not to give a hint of our dilemma to a sober person like Danny.

After a number of unsuccessful attempts, Danny's fuse finally exploded. Incorrectly believing that he was again the subject of a ball-hop, he turned the air blue with oaths. Then he proceeded homewards, sparks flying from his size 10 boots. Finally, we stumbled upon the car snugly parked in the parochial driveway.

Some distance from the town we came upon our estranged friend, pounding the tar like a marathon athlete. No amount of cajoling would entice him to travel with us – seemingly he preferred to walk the eight miles to his home.

Tooreen Hall was another popular rendezvous in those days. I was a regular attender and in fact met my wife there. I believe that I was there on the momentous occasion that the Devil made his infamous appearance.

However the aforementioned cursed drink caused me to miss the sensational event. It has become part of folk history hereabouts, though there are many variations to the telling.

I believe what happened was that a tall handsome stranger took the floor with an attractive young woman. After several dances she had become besotted with the stranger. After all, he was "devilishly handsome". The onlookers were shocked at the close manner in which he held his partner. Such a display was not commonplace in a venue run by as formidable a person as Canon Horan.

At some point during their cavorting, the lady happened to look down at his feet. Whether she saw hooves or not is speculative, but the unfortunate girl fell ill in a faint. At this point the handsome stranger ran out the door and disappeared into thin air. Now it should be noted that Tooreen Hall was heavily competing with dance promoters like the Reynolds brothers at this time. Was there in fact diabolical intervention, or maybe divine inspiration? We shall never know the truth.

Joe Keane lives with his wife in Co Mayo and since retiring has taken up creative writing as a hobby. He has had a number of his pieces published in magazines and books, including the anthologies – 'Then There Was Light' and 'Around The Farm Gate'.

Dedicated Follower
(Of The Wrong) Fashion

Lorna Sixsmith

ALTHOUGH the parish hall was in almost complete darkness, there was an air of expectancy and enthusiasm as people walked towards the porch illuminated by a single light bulb. The fluorescent strip-light along the narrow hallway beckoned them forward to the female parishioners sitting huddled in winter coats, waiting to take their admittance fees before they could go into the darkened hall.

A couple of flashing lights positioned at one end of the hall and the "One, two, one, two, testing," booming voice over the microphone provided evidence of a gathering with music. Light filtered through from the ladies toilets every time the door swung open, showing up the faded white lines of a badminton court on the wooden floor.

A visitor would be forgiven for thinking that they had stepped back in time to the 1960s – except for a few crucial details. Instead of a band, a DJ tested the sound. Everyone arrived by car rather than the mixture of cars, pushbikes and motorbikes. A scheduled break for the band and dancers for refreshments was replaced by disco-goers going into another room at any time to buy a bottle of Club Orange and a Club Milk chocolate bar.

One establishment, the Deighton Hall in Carlow, boasted a glitter ball which enlivened the decor and the atmosphere. Rather than paying an entrance fee in shillings, it was usually £2. The bouncers were male parishioners in their fifties, their wives also giving up their Friday night for this parish fundraiser. We may not have recognised them but they knew us, they knew we were our parents' sons and daughters. Stories about our clothes, our company and our behaviour may have reached home before we did. Girl's hair was either crimped to resemble crinkle cut French fries or permed to look like Sue Ellen Ewing.

While few were brave enough to copy the dress style of Cyndi Lauper or Madonna, they certainly emulated their wearing of huge earrings and noisy rattling bangles.

The monthly Church of Ireland Diocesan magazine was searched eagerly by teenagers looking for announcements of any forthcoming parish discos. No matter how far we travelled, from Carlow to Portlaoise or from Roscrea to Tinahely, the same people were almost always there. St Stephen's Night and New Year's Eve were the only nights when a large number of unknowns turned up, people home from London or Manchester for Christmas, with their new fashions and faux English accents.

If there were two discos on the same Friday night, there was consternation – which one would most people go to? No one wanted to be the sad person who went to the "wrong" one. No one wanted to drive 50 miles to arrive at a parish hall with only 20 people inside.

Of course, there were nightclubs in the 1980s too but these weren't favoured by parents. They were perceived as holding all kinds of risks. They sold alcohol, their opening on Saturday nights meant dancing into the early hours of Sundays thereby breaking the Sabbath, and they carried the risk of a mixed marriage in the future. Much better to stick to parish discos on a Friday night.

One such parish disco, in the middle of nowhere, was memorable for me – for a good reason. As the hall was some distance from any town and pubs, people arrived in dribs and drabs, four or five to a car. If it had been in a town, teenagers dropped to the hall by parents, would have gone to a local pub for half an hour first and arrived en masse at the venue later. My friends and I, chauffeured there by a friend's older brother, arrived early. The music was already blaring from the large speakers at one end with blue, red and green lights flashing on and off.

As people came in, they stood at one end of the hall until they saw others they recognised and went to greet them. As "Come on Eileen" started, four girls took to the floor while the rest of us, either more bashful or less eager to be an exhibition for all and sundry to watch, looked on with a little envy at their daring. Or perhaps we decided our sitting position was a better vantage point to view any potential strangers as they came in. We could eye up the talent as well as the competition and see how we compared to other young women with big hair, bright blue eye-shadow, heavy eyeliner and mascara, wearing high-waisted, ripped jeans with oversized t-shirts or dresses with large shoulderpads and wide belts.

"He looks nice," I thought to myself as I saw a dark-haired guy in his late teens walk across the hall. He didn't look like a farmer. Although not dressed with any great flamboyance, his clothes and haircut were a bit trendier than others in his group. At that stage in my life, I didn't want to date someone who was tied to the farm, who couldn't go on holidays, who couldn't travel, who had to milk on Sunday afternoons.

"Do you know that guy over there?" I asked a girl sitting next to me while not really expecting her to say yes?

I'm not sure why I was surprised when it turned out she was his cousin, after all, Protestant Ireland is pretty small. She proceeded to enlighten me with all his qualities chapter and verse. I was right, although he was a farmer's son, he was studying science in Dublin. He was a good cook (I was terrible, so that was welcome news); he had a baby nephew and was great at babysitting (I'd never changed a baby's nappy so this was something I recognised might come in handy in the future); and he was single.

Unfortunately, I didn't seem worthy of his attention that particular evening. Maybe my bright silver eye shadow with blue mascara wasn't sufficiently noticeable given the competition. My Dublin-bought grey leopard skin trousers and top with wide belt was perhaps too trendy for a rural disco. Maybe I should have worn bigger earrings and more bangles.

Groups of friends danced together, the more popular your group was, the bigger the circle. He stayed with his friends and I was with mine. "Careless Whisper" started the slow set. He didn't glance in my direction.

Right on schedule at 2am, the national anthem started playing and the main lights went on. Those not dancing struggled to their feet, all apart from a couple glued to each other in a dark corner. Girls wondered if their mascara was running and tentatively touched the corners of their eyes with their fingertips. As a friend and I joined a queue to collect our coats, I elbowed her and nodded across. "Do you know them?"

"I know the blond one."

"I want to chat to the other one, let's go over."

Chat she did, for about five minutes while I tried to insert the occasional intelligent statement that didn't generate much response from either of them.

I discovered many years later, that my penchant for 1980s fashion hadn't done me any favours with my future husband. Maybe my fashion sense improved as we started going out a year later when we met again at a hotel disco, not a parish hall.

Lorna Sixsmith and her husband Brian became farmers in the end, 10 years after getting married. They have a dairy and beef farm in Co Laois. Lorna has written three books 'Would You Marry a Farmer?', 'How to be a Perfect Farm Wife' and 'An Ideal Farm Husband'.

The Fight For A Fair Lady

Mark McGaugh

ALTHOUGH the two 'boyos' lived in the same parish, they had little in common. Except maybe that they loved to go to see the dance bands and they both fell madly in love with the same girl. However Martin Greally was unaware that he had a competitor in Mickey Walsh, the local auctioneer's son, for the heart of Elizabeth Jennings.

Mickey had an unenviable record when it came to how he treated the ladies, with some claims that he had a girl in tow at virtually every dance hall within a 30-mile radius of his home. Any time he was challenged on his two-timing escapades, he smirked, explained that he was a strong believer in the holy bible, and was doing his best to love his neighbours.

Somehow the news of his exploits never got to Elizabeth, maybe due to the fact that she lived in the next parish and was out of range of the gossip. Mickey stood 6'3" in his socks, weighed 14 stone and was considered one of the greatest GAA fullbacks for miles around, especially at catching the high ball.

Martin was good-looking with black wavy hair, with a touch of Brylcreem always applied for social occasions. He was a little shy and reserved, but loved music and the bands that played around his area. He was a good dancer and liked to pick a girl who was particularly nimble at doing the quickstep or the jive to get maximum pleasure out of a dance set.

A couple of weeks previously Martin had what he considered the night of his life when he had several dances with this beautiful red-haired girl. Early on that night he saw this gorgeous girl at a distance, her hair down to her slender shoulders, with a slightly freckled face, high cheekbones with pure blue eyes and air of modesty that belied her looks.

The bonus was her dancing ability and her casual smile which he found spellbinding. A great fear gripped him that he could never ask her out for a date. He also was aware that work was drying up, and like many of his friends, he might need to go to London. As a trained carpenter and joiner, he knew he could earn good money there.

He made two decisions on that Sunday evening as he was shining his black leather shoes before heading to the dance: The first was to ask Elizabeth out on a date and the second was that he would go to London and earn big money. He knew that the house and the farm would be left to his eldest brother – a very quiet and pious lad – who had worked the land for a number of years.

When he arrived into the hall that night he saw Elizabeth dancing with his nemesis, Mickey. Martin was crestfallen and even confided his thoughts to his younger sister Margaret when he got home. She worked in the bank with Elizabeth and agreed that Martin might indeed be wasting his time.

He feared in his heart that such a golden opportunity to meet and talk to her would never arise again. His friend in London, Johnny Leahy, had found him lodgings, explaining he could have his pick of work on the building sites.

Johnny met him at Euston Station and later that evening sitting on his bed in a cold room in West London, Martin had something of an epiphany. It took London for him to decide he would fight to win Elizabeth Jennings.

His father used to say: 'Faint heart never won fair lady' and now as he felt this unquenchable desire to win Elizabeth, he was indeed going to give it his best shot.

Immediately he wrote to tell her how he was settling into his new surroundings while mentioning the memory of the unforgettable night they had danced together to the sound of JJ Flynn and his band.

In the letter, he even invited her to visit London, promising he would take time off to show her the sites and the Irish dance halls.

Life, though, often gets in the way of the best laid plans. The following evening, a letter arrived from his sister Margaret indicating that his older brother, John, had decided to join the priesthood. She was giving Martin an early heads up that he might have to return home to work the farm. Scratching his jaw as he re-read the letter, he couldn't make up his mind if this news was good or bad.

Without lifting another finger, Martin's case was also boosted when it emerged that Mickey got engaged to a girl from a neighbouring county – a shock that left Elizabeth reeling.

Her drooping spirits were raised on arriving home from work when her mother motioned to the letter with a London postmark on the mantelpiece. "It looks like a man's writing," she whispered.

* * *

Several weeks later, Elizabeth travelled to London and stayed with her cousin, Nuala, who was nursing at the Queen Charlottes Hospital. Martin had been true to his word, and made himself available to show her the sites and the night spots.

Within a few days as she walked down Oxford Street with him she knew one thing for sure – the man beside her would never be the two-timing sort.

On the first night in London, Martin had told her of his strong feelings. She found that hers were reciprocating with every hour they were in each other's company. So much so that they were heading to a renowned jeweller's to choose her engagement ring.

She was an old-fashioned girl and made it clear she would not wear the sparkling diamond ring or tell anyone until Martin had returned home to ask her father for her hand in marriage.

Then they would head out with all their friends for a night's dancing – this time as an engaged couple. And yes, they'd dance till they dropped again to the sound of JJ Flynn to honour their own lovely showband romance.

Mark McGaugh is a native of Shrule, Co Mayo but emigrated to the UK in 1960. Married with three grown-up children, he retired after 40 years from business and now enjoys writing.

63

Bright Lights That Failed To Shine

Paul Holland

IN the days of sponsored radio on RTÉ around 1970, I used to hear on one particular programme that the Television Club on Harcourt St Dublin was the home of "with-it dancing" and that it was "all happening at Seezer's". I believed that Dublin must have the best social scene on earth and perhaps even in the entire Galaxy.

I envied some of my friends when they upped-sticks and departed to train at St Patrick's, Drumcondra, in Dublin as primary school teachers. Meeting them at half-term, though, I found they were a bit understated about the Dublin social scene and its bright lights. I probed them for details of night life and after some prompting, a few sad tales began to emerge. One of them told me his story, peppered with more than a few expletives, about his experiences in the capital's so-called flesh spots.

Outside one particular dancehall, he told me how he was approached by a girl who suggested: "Pay for me into the dance and I'll stay with you all night but don't expect anything else from me though".

She was very attractive and he was very lonely and the promise of a few hours company was too hard to resist. Perhaps she might relent at the end of the night and let him see her home? Hope springs eternal. However, once past the ticket desk, she disappeared into the ladies and the next time he saw his hopeful companion was when he leaned over and looked down from the heights of the balcony as she smooched cheek-to-cheek with a man in a light coloured suit.

My friend explained how he walked back to the college that night and how it started to rain along the way and how he hadn't a coat or umbrella and that his new shoes were too tight.

That started the ball rolling, now they were unashamedly sharing stories of romantic disaster. I was very discouraged by the tales they told me; walking girls home, filled with hopes of romance, only to find the courtship ended with a curt "Goodbye!" and the sound of the front door slamming in their faces.

At Carysfort Women's Teacher Training College, the girls' nights out were more curtailed. According to a friend, they were so weighed down with assignments, projects, deadlines, etc. that they had barely time to draw breath – let alone have a wild night-life. Hearing these stories I began to get worried.

But we are nothing if not creatures of optimism. I got an opportunity to see things for myself in 1972 when I spent a week in Dublin. I tried out a few dancehalls and soon it began to register with me that the reports from my friends were correct.

When I visited 'The National' in Parnell Square there seemed to be no Dublin girls present. I met girls from Cork, Westmeath, Sligo, Limerick... but no locals. A great dance – everyone was so friendly but no romance.

A few nights later, I chanced 'The Olympic Ballroom.' It was ok – maybe a bit too crowded and noisy for my liking – but basically, I thought, no real difference to dancehalls in Galway city. Where was the 'with it' magic?

Saturday night and it was time for the Television Club – the goal of my journey. The place that I had heard advertised on radio as "the home of with-it dancing." More misfortune. There was a long queue and, at the door, I was asked to show my membership card. Maybe I could have bought one – but for one night, hardly. A few friendly people in the queue told me that there would be no problem if I came on a quieter night, say a Tuesday.

I'd be home by then but I'd seen enough – the good, the bad and the indifferent. Those illuminations seem to look so much brighter when they are the lights of the imagination.

Paul Holland was born near Athenry, Co Galway in 1954. A science, maths and computer teacher for over 37 years, he now enjoys his retirement travelling all over the globe. Paul is also a keen GAA fan.

64

Hanging Out With The Rockers

Ann Lacey

I SPENT my childhood on Bray Seafront, a five minute walk from my home. The Mecca of dancing venues, The Arcadia Ballroom, was located there. My younger sister and I were too young to get in so instead spent our days nearby at the Fun Palace honing our skills.

Here, the jukebox was the centre of attraction. We liked to hang out with all the Rockers; cool, older teenagers, girls with ponytails dressed in wide skirts and tight blouses, and boys who wore drainpipe trousers and string ties like cowboys.

We, on the other hand, sported our summer outfits; ladybird shorts, hand-me-down check shirts and Clarks sandals purchased each June when my mother's shoe-club money came in. White ankle socks completed our ensemble.

It was around the Jukebox that we observed our idols and practised dancing skills for later use. We tapped our feet to the rhythm of the music when we thought no one was watching us and gazed in awe at the older teenagers actually jiving around the Jukebox. Later, at home we aped their jives in our own bedroom.

We suffered from a kind of split personality. Our bedroom walls, much to my mother's chagrin, were adorned with posters of The Beatles, The Bee Gees, The Small Faces, Gene Pitney and other international stars of the era. However, they were far removed from our orbit. Our idols were the Irish showband stars who were much more accessible. We didn't follow every band and were selective about those we liked. People like Larry Cunningham, Big Tom and Philomena Begley were dismissed as 'Culchies' as we focused our attention on Butch Moore, Eileen Reid, Dickie Rock and, of course, Brendan Bowyer, who in our eyes was definitely Elvis.

Back then I kept a book with different coloured pages, a proper 'Autograph Book'. During the summer months, my younger sister and myself parked ourselves at the stage door of the Arcadia, brimming with excitement at the expected arrival of whoever was billed for that weekend. We spent hours there and nearly always got autographs of the big stars. Often the pages read: 'To Anne, best of luck, Butch Moore' or 'To Anne with love, Dickie Rock'.

We were 10-year-old groupies before the term was invented but more importantly, we were the envy of the seafront.

Fast forward six or seven years when we parked ourselves at the front door of the Arcadia. In those years, Bray in summertime was thronged with visitors from various parts of Britain and Northern Ireland. These visitors were a source of wonder to us with their accents, beehive hairdos and sophisticated clothes. The mini-skirt was in full swing everywhere but was banned in our house.

Summer jobs were available and that provided us with a little disposable income. Where better to spend it than inside the Arcadia watching idols live on stage and experiencing the wonder of meeting 'boys'?

By now our older sister had a job and could buy lots of things that interested us. She had tubes of foundation, lipstick of different colours – we loved pink – and all sorts of lotions and potions guaranteed to make you beautiful. She also had a coveted record player. We were banned from her room but when she was at work, often we'd set ourselves up in there, ate her chocolates, go through her clothes, practice dancing and listen to her records.

When our time came to prepare for the dance where else would we go only to my sister's treasure trove? Her clothes were too big for us but our own wardrobe was limited. We probably aspired to a 'twin set,' matching jumper and cardigan, but for now we had to be content with the only outfits we possessed, a polo neck jumper and a corduroy skirt. Our outfit was completed by a pair of patent leather shoes with straps, prized possessions and most definitely a step up from the sandals. These were lovingly preserved with a slick of Vaseline every week. The ankle socks, however, had to go. What we needed were nylon stockings.

Once again we raided our sister's drawer for two pairs of her finest nylons. Inevitably, she copped on to us and I seem to recall that a lock was installed at some later stage.

Dressed to kill, wearing pink lipstick and flashing nylon stockings, we'd set out for the Arcadia. Inside the polished maple floor looked so inviting. The atmosphere was intense and everyone felt hot even before the dancing started. Upstairs a long wooden bar served gallons of lemonade and Club Orange in bottles with straws. From here the guys surveyed the talent while leaning casually on the bar counter with one elbow.

Everyone had a mini-skirt and a lot of stuffing, pulling and folding of waistbands went on in the toilets, all designed to ensure that the skirt was just the right length. There was also much jostling for mirror space. On one occasion our cue for exit arrived after a girl with a broad Dublin accented asked her companion: "Can you see my hole in this?"

When the music started the only means of communication was by head-jerking or high-pitched screams. We could 'Hucklebuck' with the best of them, but somehow we never seemed to fit in with the crowd. We were still a little too young and out of our depth.

Some years later, we would enter our prime and get on with the boys just like we had wanted to do back then. But that's another story entirely.

Anne Lacey is a retired teacher who lives in Greystones, Co Wicklow. She is a keen hill-walker and world traveller.

From Céilí
To Carnival Girl

Frances Browner

IT was 1968, and I was on my way to my first céilí. Cloghan Carnival, 14-years-old and all togged out in a purple empire-line my mother had made me. We set off up Castle Street, my cousin Alice and I, turned right at the square, which is now a roundabout, where we fell in with a few girls from the Hill Road. By the time we reached the sports field, we were a giddy group. The chat was all about which lad they had their eye on, and whether they'd 'go' with one of them later, or not. Looking back that was the best part. Down on holidays from Dublin, I clung to the camaraderie of this small Midland town.

We could hear the strain of fiddle strings, the tin whistle and piano accordion; the Kieran Kelly band warming up, luring us with their lively tunes. We could smell the turf smoke; crunch the grass under our cube heel shoes; see the Marquee soar majestic towards a royal blue sky.

We popped into the pongo tent first, to eye up the talent. For me, it was a chance to calm my nerves, for I had never chatted a boy my own age before and the place was packed with them; locals who had hovered after us through the town and strange ones from faraway.

And, I had never been 'asked up to dance.' What would I do? I lined up along the wall with the rest of the women, that's what I did, and ran every time a surge of men made for us. For men they were, aged 16 to 60 and all agog. I sought solace several times in the ladies' loo, sitting despondent on a bale of hay. "Did ya bring yer knittin'?" one chap had the nerve to roar in at me.

Alice, meanwhile, was having the time of it, twirling around the floor for the two-step; quick step; slow waltz and jive. In-and-out and in-and-out and in-and-out for the Siege of Ennis. Every time she saw my forlorn face, she gasped: "Did ya not get a dance yet?"

I was beside myself.

Finally, I found refuge in the cloakroom, where the attendant promised to mind me. I was starting to relax, even tapping my patent toes and humming along with Brendan Shine's 'Bridges of Paris' when a burly farmer shuffled forward, red-faced and freckled, a tweed cap clutched in the huge hand he proffered.

"Will ya dance?" he asked. I nudged my cloakroom companion. "Say no," she whispered. No sooner had the word fallen from my lips than he'd whisked her out onto the floor, whirling her away from me. Never saw a sign of them afterwards.

Next thing, a nice-looking fellow approached, his face shiny and hopeful, his hand clammy when he held mine and I nodded 'yes'. At the end of the set, I didn't know how to take my leave of him. He tilted his head towards the floor and we danced again, and again and again. Panic set in. After seven sets, I felt faint. Eventually, Alice ended up beside us, turned to her partner and said, "thank you."

"Thanks a million," says I to my fella who looked like he'd been hit with a hurl.

I couldn't be stopped after that. Tripping across the floorboards. Sweat streaming. Faces and lights rotating, my heart lifting with the music, falling for the National Anthem. Alice and I running home for the tea and currant cake, sitting in front of the fire, reliving dance after dance after dance.

We soon graduated onto the dancehalls and during the day, practiced our steps around the kitchen to the record-player I had hauled down on the bus. We learnt to jive to the Tremeloes 'Suddenly You Love Me' and to waltz to Larry Cunningham's 'Don't let me cross over.'

Standing on the Square, we thumbed to Birr, Ballinasloe, Athlone and Tullamore. Or piled into a hackney for two shillings, on top of another, nine or ten. Alice used to sit on the radiator in the Central Ballroom, steaming the creases out of her black bell-bottoms.

By now, I was standing bravely among the women, smiling into a sea of men, eyes downcast whenever one I didn't fancy loomed. One night, the swell parted and there stood a tall lanky lad, cobalt blue eyes and shiny brown hair. I melted into him. 'Oh, the Snakes Crawl at Night,' Hugo Duncan was singing and yer man placing his hand on the small of my back. For 'Boom-Bang-a-Bang', he pulled me closer, as the words of the song demanded, and I relented.

I inhaled the new leather of his biker jacket, his musky cologne. Felt his hair swish against my cheek, his arms strong around me. Over a mineral, he told me he worked for the ESB; a permanent, pensionable job and he not yet 18. I was the same age and about to sit my Leaving Certificate. He walked me to the car and pressed me against the bonnet for a soft kiss on the lips, my co-passengers inside shaking it from side to side.

"Be careful," Alice whispered when I squeezed in beside her. "Those motorbike types think they're great. They can get any woman they want."

I thought of him all through the exams, writing his name in the margin of every book I was supposed to be studying. Found myself back at the Carnival come July, drifting into his arms again, whenever he beckoned. Alice had kept me up to date in her weekly letters and I knew he had lots of girls after him, but they were mere shadows, ethereal, unreal. We met every night for a fortnight, and unable to settle at home, I coaxed my mother to allow me back for Birr Vintage Week in August. I was swaying nonchalantly to Johnny Regan and the Tumbleweeds in the Marian Hall, when he ambled towards me. "Hi," I said, as if I hardly knew him at all.

We danced again in Ballycumber Carnival and I was back in September for Shannonbridge, where my parents had met, and I was hoping my romance might blossom. We courted beside the river, water rustling, the moon shimmering above the bridge. He started taking me to the dances on his Honda 175, paying in for me, even offering the price of my cloakroom ticket. I was doing a line, at last.

One morning, Alice and I were wandering up the Hill Road where one of the girls announced she had 'gone' with him the previous night after he'd dropped me home. Her peat brown eyes glared at me as my heart dropped to my toes.

For nights after, I heard the Honda roar up and down Castle Street, but ignored it. By and by, I braved it into Banagher, where he sent a friend over to know what was wrong. "I'm breaking it off," I said, and watched the lad relay the message, my heart tearing in two.

All winter I lapped up Alice's letters, dying for news of him, dancing every dance alone in my bedroom. By Christmas, I was about to burst and took the train down on St. Stephens's Day in time for the County Arms.

During that holiday, in various Midland ballrooms, I caught his eye sometimes over a woman's shoulders and looked away. I also learnt the truth – he hadn't been with that other girl after all. Still, I never spoke to him again. Too much water had gone under the bridge and besides, we were now following cooler bands like the Freshmen, the Plattermen, the Conquerors and the Memories. Ah, the Memories!

It was at the céilí it all began, that first Friday night in Cloghan, and after turning up the hem of my purple empire-line, I never looked back. Sure didn't I trek 82 miles across the country by train and by bus just to meet my next heart-throb?

Frances Browner was born in Cork, grew up in Dublin, spent 20 years in New York and now resides in Wicklow. As a result, she never knows what team to shout for or what jersey to wear. Her short fiction and memoirs have appeared in 'Ireland's Own' and 'Woman's Way' and have been broadcast on RTÉ radio.

66

Back To Front For Luck!

Monica Weir

NOT every townland had a big dance hall which meant that when one of your favourite bands was playing you had a journey to and from of anything up to eight to 10 miles to hear them.

Young lads and lassies cycled, often sharing the bicycle with one sitting on the crossbar or carrier. If you were unfortunate enough to get a puncture you had to either turn back or walk fast to get to the venue. There were few cars around so the chance of a lift was slim.

Showbands left a legacy that is still warm in the hearts of those who were part of those great dancing days in Ireland. One night of that era is forever embedded in my mind. I am thinking of the time that I had just come home for the weekend and my mother – like most mothers – liked to take advantage of my presence by having plenty of chores lined up for me.

I couldn't keep my mind on the work. Brendan O'Brien and the Dixies were in the hall that night and I really wanted to go. Over a cuppa my mother told me that my brother was also due home. Well, my heart skipped a beat because I knew he would definitely be going. Just then I remembered that my lovely green jumper was not terribly clean so I gave it a quick wash and hung it out on the clothesline to dry.

There was a spring in my step as I got the lavender polish and cloth to polish the landing and stairway to keep my mother happy.

Then the dog started to bark which meant my brother was home. He said that his friend was bringing his car and when I asked if I could have a lift, he replied: "I suppose you can".

My jumper was not fully dry so I draped it over a chair in front of the open fire. I then finished the cleaning and began to help with the supper. Afterwards I washed up the dishes and put them away before washing myself. I took out my lovely A-line skirt. It was really smart. Then I ran downstairs to get my jumper. To my horror I saw a big scorch mark on the upper half of the front. I nearly died!

There was no way I could go to the dance as it was the only one I had with me. My heart sank all the way down to my toes. My mother must have felt sorry for me because she took the jumper from me and declared: "It's fine. All you have to do is put it on back to front – sure it's your front they will be looking at and your hair will cover the scorch at the back."

I gave her a kiss on the cheek in relief before running upstairs. I dressed quickly, took a look in the mirror and decided everything was perfect.

By that time the dog was barking again as the Prefect pulled into the yard. Full of excitement and with my new ankle boots on, I waved goodbye to mother. When I got to the car, I could see that it was already full. I took a quick step backward when one of the lads said: "Climb in here and you can sit on someone's knee". My brother then squeezed in beside another fella in the front passenger's seat and off we went singing and joking as only the young can do.

My brother paid the admission for me while I paid for a cloakroom ticket. When I took off the coat I held my head up and backward to ensure my hair was covering the scorch mark.

When the band started playing there was an almighty stampede across the floor. I forgot about the head position as I was pulled out onto the floor. The music was electric. The atmosphere was intoxicating. Some of the lads had a few pints to rid them of shyness while unfortunately some others had a few too many which rid them of their senses.

After a short break my brother took me out for a fast jive. We had to jostle our way to get some space. I asked if the scorch mark was very visible. "Well," he said, "you're moving so fast no one will see it". He was right. I was flying but then I missed his hand and landed on my bum. I was like a spinning wheel careering out of control down the floor – bringing a few couples down with me on the way.

A young gentleman caught me before I hit the wall. As he helped lift me up, he inquired if I was okay, then asked if I had brushed against something as I had a yellowish mark on the back of my jumper? I felt the blood rush to my face but before I could answer, my brother changed the subject by declaring: "You were fairly moving there."

He then told the young man to finish the dance with me, claiming I would be in safer hands. From then on I totally forgot all about the big scorch mark. Or that I was wearing my jumper back to front. I was about to have a night to remember!

Monica Weir is a native of Roscommon where she lives among her 12 grandchildren. She enjoys writing short stories and children's stories as a main hobby now that her family is reared.

67

Falling Into The Wrong Hands

Seán Burns

GROWING up in the 1940s and 50s along the north Louth border was a very different world to today. Smuggling was routine for many during and after the Second World War, and was almost acceptable as a legitimate means of earning a living. If the smuggling was going well, you might be able to afford a car and that made a big difference to your social life.

The Sunday night dance was the highlight of the week for most young, and not so young, around that area. However, the general behaviour at country dances had to pass the moral views of the parish priest. Sometimes the man of the cloth might nip in behind the stage to check that all was above board. Close dancing and jazz (God forbid) were severely frowned on.

The dance halls in the larger towns were different. The skirts were shorter, cigarettes were openly smoked by the more daring women, the music was from the pop charts; all very distasteful to the local guardians of morality.

My wife to be, Liz, and I were regular dance-goers. We were usually accompanied to the local dances by my younger brother, Brian, who was often the driver and another one or other of our pals, who hitched a lift with us in my father's Fiat 1500.

We had a slightly older male friend who often came with us as well. He was tight with money and never contributed to the petrol for the trip, but he was good crack and gave us plenty of laughs, so we didn't mind too much.

One Sunday night, The Royal Show Band – his favourite – was playing at the new Adelphi Ballroom in Dundalk, so of course we had to go. Michael, our pal, was in excellent form as he had just got his hay cut that day. With a bit of luck he would get it turned and maybe baled the following evening. Sometimes Liz would stay over in my parent's house after a dance, as she lived outside Banbridge but worked as a nurse down the road from us in Newry.

Michael assumed that she would be staying at our house that night and when he heard we had to leave her home, his mood changed. The drive involved a 40-mile round trip, taking up to two hours. This meant Michael wouldn't see bed until 4am – and him with a big hay-making day on the horizon.

After a bout of calling us the worst names he could come up with, he calmed down as we reached the glitzy new ballroom in Dundalk.

After queuing for an age, we finally got to the cash desk, where our pal Michael received another major shock, the 7/6 fee. Inside, the hall was packed and he began to moan that we should have gone somewhere else. Suddenly he let out a curse: "Jaysus, I left the bloody loft door open, the 'hins' will be out and the fox will get them all!"

The night hadn't started well – but worse was to come.

We lost sight of Michael for a while but when we all caught up again, he was in much better form. "Oh Seán, I met this lovely girl," he confided. "She's been dancing very close up to me." With that, he disappeared into the crowd again. The music was terrific and we didn't notice the time passing, until a good bit later Michael appeared again – with a very red face – and sheepishly told us the reason for it.

"After we had a dance, I invited her for a mineral and while we were sipping our Club oranges, the music stopped and next thing didn't Brendan Bowyer step forward to sing Boulavogue."

Now, Michael was a huge fan so he took his new partner's hand and made his way through the crowd closer to the stage. Finally, he found a good position and brimming with excitement, he gave his partner's hand a squeeze of endearment.

The strength of the squeeze he got back surprised him and on turning, he discovered that he had been holding the hand of a rather large, confused looking chap instead of the girl.

He belted off the dance floor as quickly as he could and grabbed us on the way.

Not unexpectedly, he wasn't too keen to go back to The Adelphi for a long time after that. Of course we laughed ourselves sick at his little adventure and we never let him forget it, especially when he was on a rant, giving out about the price of minerals or dance tickets.

We continued going to the dances with Michael for many years, but somehow after that night, whenever he heard Boulavogue again, he made sure to see whose hand he was holding.

Seán Burns was born Carrickarnon on the north Louth border. He is married to Liz and has a family of six. He retains a great interest in history and politics.

Tunnels, Skeletons And Wellington Boots

Victor Sandilands

DURING my time working in the tunnels of the Victoria Line in 1960s London, all I could think about was getting dressed and going to the Galtymore on a Saturday night.

When you entered the dance, it felt like you were going home. There was plenty of craic and you even found out who was paying the best rates for the 'lump'. I always felt sadness when the band stopped playing at the end of the night and you had to face reality again.

At one time, I was working at the Barbican with Turriff Construction. They were contracted to remove all the bones from a graveyard. We had to tie the bones up with string and place them in wheelbarrows to take them to the site offices for the local Council. We had some macabre fun chasing each other with bones and putting them into older men's lunch boxes.

While we lived in Leeds we used to travel to The Astoria Ballroom in Manchester to see a 'townie' singer John Kerr.

He and Robert Ward used to own and run the Mulroy Ballroom in Kerrykeel, Co Donegal and across Mulroy Bay the Gallagher Bros owned Gallagher's Ballroom in Carrigart which attracted massive crowds until The Fiesta Ballroom opened in Letterkenny.

That was the first place I saw strobe lighting, where everything in white lit up – even my mate James Louge's shirt collar. James and I travelled miles on our bicycles to the dances. He didn't have money for a chain for his bicycle, so we lowered the saddle so he could use his feet to help me pull him with a rope.

The farmer's wife that James worked for used to hide his shoes on Fridays and Saturdays, thinking it would stop him from going to 'The Hop' as he called it. She used to tell him the dance halls were the devil's houses, claiming that his shoes should be for going to Mass and nothing else.

We cycled long distances to those dances.

At the hops I often dared James to ask a good-looking girl up but the girls would hide when they saw him coming. With his shoes imprisoned by the farmer's wife, everyone at the dance could see that he was wearing wellingtons under the legs of his trousers. And if they didn't see them, they certainly heard them slapping against the backs of his legs as he walked across the floor.

After refusing poor old James, I'd head for the good-looking girl and more often than not she would be relieved to accept.

It was all great craic in Ireland's dancehalls and the Galtymore was the same for those exiled in the English capital. It was as if every young Irish person had a magnet pulling them to the Galtymore.

After we moved to the Highlands of Scotland, 40 years ago, every St Patricks Day we would either go down to London to spend Saturday at the Ideal Homes Exhibition at Earls Court before heading on the Paddy's Night to the Galtymore. It was like a home from home.

When I say to people we would go a 1,000 miles for a dance, well, that has happened quite a few times, such as going from Slochd to the Galtymore and on a number of occasions driving five hours to the ferry at Stranraer, cross over to Larne and then drive across to Kane's in Oranmore to see Declan Nerney or even to Limerick or Wexford for a dance before heading back home on the Sunday in time for work on Monday.

Shortly after the Galtymore was demolished, we were visiting relations in London and went to see the remains of the iconic dancehall – there was a carwash business on part it. If every Irishman and Irishwoman in the UK donated a £5, I'm sure a grand Galtymore could be rebuilt. Who's up to donating the first fiver?

Victor Sandilands is a native of Ramelton, Co Donegal but emigrated to London when he was 19. Married and still an avid dance fan, his other hobbies include cycling and going home to Ireland for weekends.

Something In The Air

PJ Cunningham

T HUNDERCLAP NEWMAN'S hit song of that year had predicted that there was "Something in the Air". And that night, Sunday July 20, 1969 and indeed for much of the small hours of the next morning, that 'something' would be defined in dramatic circumstances on two fronts.

Apollo 11 had manoeuvred its way beyond the earth's atmospheric pull into space so that – all things going well – it was only hours from landing on the moon. RTÉ advertised that it would be televising the event through the night.

As fate would have it, there was also something major happening in our corner of the world – a new disco dance was being run in the parochial hall. The 'Disco-Go-Go,' was an even bigger deal for the town's young denizens than prospects of a moon landing.

The disco began at 10pm but the cool dudes like my friend and myself decided we should wait until about half eleven to make our entry. I called for him just after eleven and as we walked the half mile to the hall, our eyes scanned the sky. Passing the Fire Station we examined the bright moon to see if we could detect even the slightest of movement. We couldn't.

The sky presented itself as something funky that night. Twinkling stars surrounded the lantern moon, while the shadows created by low-passing cloud had, as Joni Mitchell put it, "feather canyons everywhere."

Something in the air! Inside the disco, the theme of darkness being penetrated by flashing lights was even more accentuated. There was a feeling of hidden-layers of depth and the louche of theatrical spaciousness. It offered momentary snapshots – like a photographer's camera flash – of a heaving dance floor contorting to the Rolling Stones' newest hit 'Honky Tonk Woman'.

The sound, the buzz, the vibrations flirted seductively with the senses right around this new-fangled 'Disco-Go-Go'. Circular lights flicked colours sequentially – red, orange and blue onto the walls. The dazzling shaft tattooed the dancers momentarily with alien-like silhouettes that changed with the beat on the dance floor.

The inter-galactic motif was punctuated by the interspersing white flashes flooding down from the ceiling's overhead projections in swirling abstract patterns.

Only the impediment of two left feet and a tendency to dance best from the shoulder up could restrict a young buck on such a night. And unfortunately, that was my lot as I surveyed the scene in front of me.

Slicker in the rules of getting someone up to dance, my friend slinked like a plume of smoke into the iridescent glitter near the stage and emerged with a girl clad in a short white dress.

The thud, thud, thud of the music made it hard to hold conversations but whatever he whispered in her ear, she immediately exploded into laughter, all the while shaking her head to the rhythm of the record.

When he came back, his jet black hair was stuck to his face. "It's like an oven out there," he said, nodding to where he had just been. He took out a 10-pack of Major, lit a cigarette and after taking a drag out of it, threw it in my direction. He then lit up another for himself.

The cigarette smoke drifted upwards like dry ice, creating a blue haze canopy above the dance floor.

The music began again with Tommy Roe's 'Dizzy.' My head was spinning too! Yet the more I watched lads who were no good at football looking smooth and adroit on the dance floor, the more convinced I became that I'd let the first night pass without joining in.

My logic was that no dance and therefore no refusal would be better to take home to bed than the mortification of being turned down... and replaying it a thousand times in my head before sleep brought temporary respite.

"Come on, you grab the one I had the last time and I'll get her sister up?" my friend ordered as he stomped out his cigarette butt.

I let him away on his own. The girl acquiesced to his outstretched arm and it was only when he was making moves on the floor that he noticed I was still sitting in the same place. His expression showed bewilderment and maybe a hint of disgust at my reluctance.

When he came back, he used his shirt sleeves to wipe the sweat from his forehead.

FROM THE CANDY STORE TO THE GALTYMORE

"They won't come and ask you, you know," he said with a smile on his face and an edge to the tone of his voice.

I nodded in embarrassed understanding.

I went for a mineral to pass the time and to avoid being mistaken for a male version of a wallflower. I visited the gents three times and once, just once, I inched my way closer to the amplifiers at the stage front to see if I could hear more clearly the words of Zager and Evans new song: 'In the year 2525.'

I couldn't and was still trying to work out what age I might be in that year when the DJ shocked my senses by calling the last set.

Within minutes, the National Anthem had been played and the main lights were switched back on. In the harsh illumination, the imagination of the dark's shimmering shadows evaporated – for another week anyway.

By then, it was well beyond two o'clock and time to go home.

My friend stayed further up the hall. Then a petite girl with a cute Cleopatra hairstyle emerged from the ladies toilet and went up to him as she slung a shawl over her shoulders.

They headed in my direction. He introduced her to me even though I had often met her before on the streets. "Oh, I know you," she said in a teasingly friendly voice.

In the absence of knowing what to do, I thought the best thing might be to say 'goodnight' and head home on my own.

Then she piped up again: "It's not every day I've a man either side serenading me to my door. C'mon, let's go."

As we began walking, my friend put his arm around his conquest.

She was bubbly and engaging and included me in the chit-chat. She sang over and over again the title line of Three Dog Night's song 'One (is the loneliest number),' then laughed: "I wonder where that leaves three – as in us?"

I wondered too. Approaching her house, I stalled a little to allow them go on ahead. At her gate, they kissed and I parked myself as insouciantly as I could against her neighbour's railing some yards away.

After a short time, she looked in my direction and beckoning with her index finger, commanded: "C'mere you."

For a second I glanced behind me, thinking that maybe it was someone else she was addressing.

"It's you," she smiled whimsically, her eyes dancing under the street's yellow light.

My friend lit up another fag and made his way out in the middle of the road as I approached her – my head spinning again.

* * *

"Was that your first?" she whispered afterwards?

I nodded awkwardly.

She squeezed my hands gently and then let go. She turned towards my pal and gave him a second kiss before sending us both home on our way.

At that very moment there was something in the air –it was me. My feet didn't touch the ground for the rest of the short journey home.

I told my friend I was tired and refused his invitation for tea and a chat. In reality, I wanted to jump into bed and rewind until dawn that experience...my first kiss.

However, I was shocked to find my father still up in the kitchen when I entered. My face flushed and I immediately used the back of my hand to swipe my mouth in case there was a hint of lipstick.

"Anything wrong?" I asked defensively.

"No, but I couldn't go to bed until I see if man lands on the moon. They're nearly there," he added, as he pointed towards the television which was flicking out black and white images across the kitchen table.

"Put the kettle on and we'll see if they get there before it's time to get the cows in to milk."

As we sat drinking tea and eating brown bread with slabs of creamy butter on top, Neil Armstrong slowly – very slowly – as the clock neared four o'clock in the morning, journeyed on the lunar landing module, Eagle. Buzz Aldrin was in his slipstream and the man with the Irish name, Michael Collins, drew the short straw and was left to twiddle his thumbs back in the mother ship. I wondered how he kept himself occupied during his lonely vigil. Hopefully he had a first kiss to look back on!

Reflections on mine would have to wait until Armstrong put foot on the lunar landscape. I wished he'd hurry up but everything in the moon's atmosphere played out in slow motion.

The snowy reception on our Pilot TV and the crackling interruptions as the astronauts talked the 240,000 miles through space back to earth, added to the sense of time-lagging.

There was now literally a man on the moon. Armstrong's voice underlined the startling fact, declaring that the occasion would be remembered as "one small step for man, one giant leap for mankind."

Time and space...just like my walk towards the girl an hour before. Then it had happened; she pulled my head down and landed her lips on mine. A first kiss.

Now this had happened – a man walking on the moon – and 600 million people worldwide had witnessed it.

My father shook his head in disbelief. "There's a night that'll live with us forever," he said aloud as he turned off the television.

"For sure," I said, knowing full well we were talking about two totally different subjects as we headed upstairs to bed.

PJ Cunningham is a writer and editor who lives in Bray, Co Wicklow.
A native of Clara, Co Offaly, he is married with five grown-up children and is a keen sports fan, particularly of the GAA.

70

Friday Night At The Fiesta

Moira Gallagher

Running up the ballroom steps
my feet are tapping,
keeping time to the music from inside.
Queue to pay 7/6d at the box office,
turn right into the ladies cloakroom,
rummage in bag for hairspray and lipstick.
After a quick fix at the crowded mirror,
coat and bag exchanged for cloakroom ticket
which I tuck into shoe for safekeeping
Let the magic begin.
Through the rows of ladies
waiting to be asked to dance
I wind my way to the right hand corner
near the stage --the Carrigart corner.
It's here the friends from our area assemble
and the boys we know will find us easily
in this huge mass of swaying bodies.
Oh, please make John Joe be here tonight.
My eyes are out on stalks
trying to find him in the crowd.
Would you like to dance?
Some stranger;
must not refuse, it's impolite.
And so it goes, dance after dance,
answering the same questions over and over.
"Do you come here often?"
"What do you think of the band?"
"Would you like a mineral?"
This you must refuse as to accept
would imply a commitment.

Oh, where is John Joe?
Then I spot him, his long black hair
Just like the Beatles, so very handsome.
He is jiving with someone,
All I notice is the beautiful dress
Billowing as she twirls around.
"Your next dance please"
John Joe and beautiful dress head
for the mineral bar.
I watch them with sinking heart.
Hope dies.
yet the glittering ball in the middle of the ceiling
goes on twinkling and turning.
Keep that smile plastered on your face,
Pretend you don't care,
forget about the unfaithful Beatle
You might meet someone special tonight.
Time wears on,
lights are turned down for slow dances.
All too soon the band announces
"Take your partners for the last dance, please"
Post mortem with friends next day,
I say that it was a great night
while quietly listening to more exciting reports
of who met up with whom
and of further dates planned.
Just one thing I know for sure
that next Friday night at eleven o clock
I'll be running up the Fiesta steps again
Feet tapping to the music
and bubbling with anticipation
that maybe this will be THE night.

Moira Gallagher is a native of Creeslough, but now lives in Lifford, Co Donegal. She is a retired teacher who writes stories and poems as a hobby.

71

The Lovely Grá Mo Chroí

Joe McShane and Margo O'Donnell

I travelled with my country band from the dear old Emerald Isle
Through Scotland, Wales and England we sure put up the miles
This song I sing for you tonight is about a certain show
My band and I were playing at the famous Galtymore*

That night as I was walking in London's city fair
I heard a voice call out my name and saw him lying there
Just another homeless man and shabby clothes he wore
Then he told me a story that shook me to the core

He said "the curse of drink came ore me and stole my youth away
Now my bed is cardboard boxes at the closing of the day
I once stood strong and tall, you know, and earned an honest pay
But now I long for Ireland much more than words can say."

Chorus

Please sing a song of Ireland so I can picture home
Before my childhood faded and a boy began to roam
Leaving Mom and Dad behind who loved me tenderly
So sing that song for me tonight, the lovely grá mo chroí

To see my country man like this so sad and so alone
I couldn't walk away that night, this man had touched my soul
Then I invited him to come and listen to the show
As I felt the hand of God take us both across the road

I clasped your hand in friendship and sang that song for you
I could see your time on earth was short and I knew what I must do
So I took you home to Ireland just to be there for a while
And I laid you down to rest my friend beneath the Irish soil

Chorus

I sang a song of Ireland so you could picture home
Before your childhood faded and a boy began to roam
Leaving Mom and Dad behind who loved you tenderly
So here's a song for you tonight, the lovely grá mo chroí

Bridge

You became my dearest friend and as I stand here by your grave
I'll sing another song you loved at the close of an Irish day.

** (Poetic licence, as it wasn't actually The Galtymore but outside a Catholic
Club between Hammersmith and Fulham that Margo met this man).*

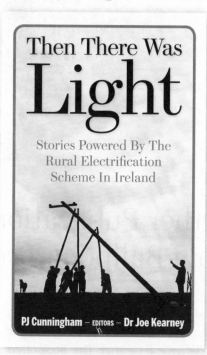
Then There Was Light

Then There Was Light is a collection of stories set against a backdrop of the Rural Electrification Scheme's roll-out across the country 70 years ago.

The stories, from eye-witnesses, ESB employees and the general public offer a rare glimpse into the Ireland of that time. They also outline the challenges faced in implementing arguably the greatest social revolution ever experienced in the country.

The accounts capture the tension that arose between old Ireland and the making of the new. Some people embraced the scheme enthusiastically while others declared that electrification could "blow up everyone in their own beds."

Available at all good book shops and also from ballpointpress.ie or email ballpointpress1@gmail.com

Other Publications from Ballpoint Press

Around The Farm Gate is a unique collection of 50 stories about rural Irish life set at the crossroads between tradition and modernity in the latter part of the twentieth century. This book offers a rare glimpse of recent Irish history, encapsulating and preserving the traditions of several generations in a rapidly disappearing rural landscape.

A Fly Never Lit is the third in a trilogy of memoirs by author PJ Cunningham about rural life in Ireland from the 1960s and 1970s. It follows on from *The Lie Of The Land*, which was published in 2013, and *The Long Acre*, published in 2014, which was shortlisted for the Bord Gáis Energy Irish Book Awards for Irish Book Of The Year.

A Fly Never Lit examines the characters and events of a changing Ireland of that time. It is written with the keen perception of an eye-witness carefully watching and listening as someone clearly fascinated by the flow of 'ordinary plenty' in the daily life of rural Ireland.

To order any of the above books, visit www.ballpointpress.ie or email ballpointpress1@gmail.com